# The World Needs Your Hustle

# PRAISE FOR
## *THE WORLD NEEDS YOUR HUSTLE*

"A lot of people write about hustle; Kevin actually does it! We could all learn something from his unique, honest, creative outlook on what it takes to really make things happen!"

**– JON ACUFF**
*New York Times* Bestselling Author of *Do Over*

"There are people who have dreams, and there are people who actually do something with those dreams. Kevin is one of the rare ones who hustles and gets things done. If you're feeling stuck, unmotivated, or maybe like you don't even have a dream, *The World Needs Your Hustle* may be just the thing to help you take that leap and make your dreams a reality. After all, the world really does need your hustle."

**– CORIE CLARK**
Author of *The Simplicity Project* &
Creator of *The Purposeful Planner*®

"A book should be a surprise. Kevin's book is a delightful surprise, full of fun and challenge. Best of all, it could change your world."

**– MIKE LOOMIS**
Coach and Writer, MikeLoomis.co

"For those of us who find ourselves standing with fistfuls of hopes and dreams yet paralyzed by the unknown, *The World Needs Your Hustle* is a roundhouse kick in the rear end. From the first few pages, it's clear that Kevin understands what drives us as human beings - the innate need for purpose and connection, to know that we matter. And as a goal coach, he has a wonderful sense of how we get in the way of ourselves. Short and sweet for good reason, Kevin provides actionable intel on how to stop waiting and start working."

### – BEN MORTON
Writer, JBenMorton.com


"Kevin Buchanan hits all the right pressure points of why pursuing your passion is selfless. I dare you to read *The World Needs Your Hustle* and not get fired up about a dream lying dormant in your heart."

### – BETHANY JETT
Author of *The Cinderella Rule: A Young Woman's Guide to Happily Ever After*

# The World Needs Your Hustle

## Make Your Goals and Dreams Matter

Kevin Buchanan

Cover Design by Devan Vannarsdall
Edited by Bethany Jett and Ronei Harden
Book Design by James Woosley (JamesWoosley.com)

ISBN: 978-0-692-64251-1

# DEDICATION

This book is dedicated to my sisters, Christy and Cara.
Throughout the years the strength of our sibling relationship
has proven time and time again to be unbreakable. I am
grateful for your endless encouragement and strong belief in
my life. Maybe one day the world will watch our reality show
and realize we are the funniest people on the face of the
planet! Love you both!

# CONTENTS

# THE WORLD NEEDS YOUR HUSTLE

The world needs your hustle.
It needs your dreams, your goals, your vision.
It needs the gifts you have been given,
unique and meant to be expressed.
The world needs your hustle.
It needs your ideas, your faith in the unknown,
your hope for a better life.
It needs you to be YOU.
My friend, your hustle matters
because the world matters.
The world needs your hustle.
The road is long.
Doubts and fears will crowd your mind.
Remember *why* you hustle and
*who* your life could change.
Let the passion to serve be your inspiration and
strength to see the journey through.
Dream. Sacrifice. Commit.
Rise early; stay up late.
Do whatever it takes to make your dreams happen.
Take your next step
Because the world needs your hustle.

– Kevin Buchanan

# INTRODUCTION

I usually decide within the first five minutes of viewing a movie whether I will continue to watch it or not. Which means, if we go to the movies together, we need to arrive early and not miss the first five minutes!

In fact, I love watching the previews, so being late is not an option. If we walk into the theater after the house lights go down, we might as well turn around and go home. My night is ruined, which means your night is ruined.

Who's ready for a movie date with me?

Similar to the first few notes of a musical score, the introduction of the film's characters affects our senses and emotions. It's so important to the rest of the story.

As a writer, there is so much pressure on the opening

sentence. Will the readers like it? Will they love it? Will they want to keep reading? Will they want to actually spend their hard-earned money and purchase it?

The struggle is real, folks.

And yet, here you are, taking this journey with me. I'm grateful.

## SURVEY TIME

Let me ask you a few questions:

Are you satisfied with where your life is right now?

Does your job give you a feeling of purpose?

Are your days predictable?

When you hear of new and exciting things going on in the world, do you immediately think, "That is great for them, but not for me. I will just stay wrapped up in my own little Snuggie® world and not venture out."?

If you said "yes," we need to talk.

Are you telling me that you choose to live your days cramped inside four uncomfortable walls, eating the same tired Ramen noodles, and watching the same mindless shows day after day, all the while, there is a city that never sleeps happening right outside your door?!?

Get out of the apartment!

Get out!

Live life!

If the idea of dreams, goals, and finding your purpose

in life is overwhelming, this is definitely the book for you.

However, if the idea of dreams and goals and purpose in life turns you off, then you might want to look for that receipt.

And in addition to reevaluating your purchase, you might want to reevaluate your life.

Ouch! Did I say that out loud?

I sure did, but some moments in life hurt, don't they?

My girl Beyoncé says, "Pretty hurts." I say, "So does the truth." But yes, my friend, the truth sometimes hurts.

If you are content with average and want nothing more out of life than to slowly become permanently etched into your couch, I challenge you to get intentional with your life. I mean, let's face it—you aren't getting off that couch anyway, so you might as well.

Now that I am working on issuing refunds to some of you, let me chat with the go-getters.

If you are *not* content with where your life is right now–

If you want something new–

If you have failed at accomplishing goals–

If you are tired of the routine and want to shake things up a bit–

If you know that your life is meant for more–

If you need to be reminded why your life matters–

…why your dreams matter,

…then keep reading!

Rip that receipt into shreds and throw it in the air like

glitter at a Gaga concert, because together we are going to explore this crazy thing called life and discover the importance of living out our dreams, accomplishing our goals, and being our true, authentic, original, creative, one-of-a-kind self!

## DREAM, PEOPLE!

What is your dream for your life?

We throw that word around a lot. I guarantee you will see that word several times in this book! Why use the word "dream"? Doesn't it conjure up feelings of something outside our own reality, something beyond our grasp?

Yes, it does, but that is exactly why I like it so much. We are meant to do what is outside of our immediate grasp. It might seem outside the realm of our own perspective of reality. That is what makes it so captivating! Our dreams have an alluring charm that we cannot escape.

I believe we are all meant for greatness. There are thousands, if not millions, of ways for greatness to be expressed. We are created to live out the best possible life we can.

We have to put in the work. It provokes us to seek after more.

# UNEXPECTED GREATNESS FROM SMALL YESES

I want to be the male Oprah. Is this out of the reach of reality? Maybe. But watch out. I've already been nicknamed "Moprah" so we'll see.

In June of 2013, I responded to an email from Jon Acuff, a New York Times best-selling author, that said "Do you want to go on an adventure?."

I said yes.

Little did I know, saying yes to one little email would change my life.

Jon is the author of five books, including *Quitter*, *Start*, and *Do Over: Rescue Monday, Reinvent Your Work, and Never Get Stuck*. He has worked with many national brands including The Home Depot, Bose, and Staples. He has a crazy amount of followers on social media, has been featured on national television, and has spoken to hundreds of thousands of people across the globe.

This wasn't some random "Jon" asking if I wanted to go on an adventure. That would be awkward. This was someone I had been following for awhile and I was interested in the kind of life he lived.

That email not only asked if I wanted to go on an adventure, he later followed up and asked me to join a Facebook group called "Dreamers and Builders." The group is comprised of people from around the world who want to be doing more with their life. They aren't satisfied with average. They want something more...something different.

They are a group of encouragers who want more than living a daydream. They are about building and making it happen.

I was instantly drawn to these strangers who thought like me. People who knew what they wanted but desperately needed a community of other like-minded individuals to share with, to bounce ideas off of, and to eventually celebrate successes with!

Out of that group, Jon started another project and formed a sub-group called the "30 Days of Hustle."

This is where things got real for me.

Members of the 30 Days group were challenged even more to put action to their words. For thirty days, we received daily email challenges showing us how to make progress, to sacrifice, and to truly hustle on our goals and dreams.

I became actively involved in this group and still am today. It allows me to express my gifts in ways I never thought possible. As the 30-Day Challenge started, I decided that I would get up every morning at 5:00 AM to hustle on my writing goals.

As the months continued, I found myself inspired by the variety of people who were working on their goals and dreams. Thousands of people from around the world were working on so many different things, and we all knew it would take lots of hustle to get the job done.

I wanted to encourage them even more, so I wrote a poem entitled, "The World Needs Your Hustle," the same poem found in the front of this book. I remember sitting at my table and writing it out, revising it a couple of times, and then posting it to the 30 Days group.

I asked my best friend Rachel Mayo to create an artistic rendering of the poem. She did, and people began buying the print to hang up in their offices and homes as a reminder of why they were hustling after their dreams.

I had no idea one post in a Facebook group would connect with so many. People shared how they stopped viewing their goal as insignificant. They began to understand that what they wanted for their life wasn't only for them. They had to do it. The hustle took on a deeper meaning.

I loved how people were making the same connections I had.

Out of the Dreamers and Builders group came the Launch Out conference in June of 2014 that propelled me even further in my dream. Held in Tulsa, Oklahoma, it was a chance for those of us in the group to actually "do" our dream.

I couldn't pass up the opportunity to meet these dreamers and builders in real life! I wanted to speak at the conference, so I chose to expand the poem into a presentation.

It was my chance to look each of these inspiring people in the eye and tell them why they should continue hustling in life. They motivated me to do more with my life in ways they could not imagine, and I aspired to do the same for them.

I wanted the chance to say how awesome it was to see them take intentional steps and live out their dreams. To watch the truth sink in that their hustles meant something even more. To observe them connecting with the idea that others depended on them living out their authentic lives!

As I spoke, I noticed the light bulb click with so many of them. Oh, they were already hustling but connecting that hustle to the bigger reason of *why* turns on an even brighter light. It was an amazing weekend that turned into a conference and continues to grow every year! If you get the chance to attend a Launch Out conference, do it!

From the conference came the passion to write this book. I wanted the opportunity to encourage even more people that their lives mattered, that their dreams mattered, and to understand the importance of living that out now.

So, that's why this book found its way into your hands. Jon Acuff hustled; I wrote this book.

A community of online dreamers inspired me to do more with my life; I wrote this book.

I connected with the truth that others need me to live out my dreams. I hope you will be moved to live out yours.

# BONUS INTRODUCTION

Have you ever felt that you were meant to do more?

Is there a passion you have neglected, a purpose that is such a part of you that it is in your DNA, but it has been buried so deep by life that you wonder if it will ever make it back to the surface?

What about goals?

Do you love or hate that word? Maybe the idea of goals makes you want to pull your hair out because you never seem to accomplish one. If that's you, make a goal to finish reading this book. Success!

I have a friend that always uses responses like "I want to punch you in the throat right now" when I start talking about goals. He is a good friend, but clearly he does not have good feelings about the G word. He has issues, bless him.

I get it. January 1st rolls around and people start blabbing about resolutions and goals, *blah blah blah...eye roll.*

Well stop it. I'm one of those "weirdos," as you like to refer to them, that are fanatics about January 1st. It is second to Christmas. It is a fresh canvas, a blank slate with perfectly squared open calendar spaces ready to be filled in with greatness.

I love goals and the moment of accomplishment which always leads to a happy dance! That alluring charm gets me every time.

If you aren't sold on goals yet, don't write me off. But let's focus on the goal-setters, the lovers of the world, really.

You know *exactly* which goals to set. You know the dreams for your life, but you may be too scared to take that first step. Perhaps you break out in a cold sweat at the very thought of stepping out into the unknown. It might be happening now. Just don't sweat on these pages, okay? The words are too pretty for that.

Or maybe you aren't sure what goals to set. Perhaps you aren't sure if you have a dream for your life, but you know the life you are living now needs *more.*

You don't have to settle for average. You are ready for more. You need it. Your goals and dreams already exist...they have been there all along. We simply need to do a little decluttering to find them.

Maybe you used to know the dream. You used to set goals. Then life happened and everyone else drained your energy and focus; that dream you once had seems to have been buried deep within your past.

The good news is that it's never fully gone. It can resurface and make a fabulous comeback in your

> **What if we were able to grasp the fact that there is a much bigger reason for why we should live out our dreams?**

life complete with jazz hands and everything! And who doesn't love a good comeback? Especially with jazz hands!

No matter where you are on your journey, there is hope! Yay! And part of that hope comes in the form of an eleven-letter word called P-E-R-S-P-E-C-T-I-V-E. Go ahead, and count them. What if I told you that there was another way of looking at it? What if we were able to grasp the fact that there is a much bigger reason for why we should live out our dreams!

Ahh, it is happening! I feel the warm fuzzies coming. Kind of like hugging a Care Bear for the first time. Group hug everyone!

Here's the truth.

I believe that our lives matter. That we were created for

a reason...for a multitude of reasons. Call it purpose, gift, strengths, whatever you want. But there are times in life when we are doing something and we know in that moment that we are doing what we were created to do.

Have you ever had that happen? It ignites something inside us that makes us feel alive. Our heart beats a little faster, our bodies awaken, and the little hairs on the back of our neck stand up. We are living the life we were meant to live.

We all want more of that.

Now, I am not talking about a "live every day like it is your last" kind of word vomit. No. That stuff is ridiculous and makes me puke in my mouth a little when I hear people say it.

Other examples of word vomit would be...

"You will find that special someone when you stop looking." (Blech!)

"Do what you love and you will never work a day in your life." (Gag!)

And my favorite - "#blessed."

I just hurled all over the floor!

Can we all agree to stop using these phrases and simply make the world a better place, please?

I am talking about *real life* people. The kind of life where what we do really matters. Where we are able to connect to the truth inside of us which then allows our authentic selves to be fully expressed in the world. It is about connecting with others and working together. This thought is both exhilarating and mind-blowing to me!

Yes, there are parts of life that are mundane. Paying bills, cleaning house (I love it though), going to the grocery store, and for me, yard work. Cleaning out the lint trap is also mundane, but after I went ten months without cleaning mine, my dryer wasn't working and my mom was amazed that I hadn't burnt my first apartment to a crisp. Lesson learned. Check the lint trap.

There are the things we have to do day in and day out that are simply not fun. But even in those moments, we know we are working towards the greater good. I believe we all crave purpose, connection, and need to know that we matter.

You matter.

---

# I believe we all crave purpose, connection, and need to know that we matter.

---

Who wants to go through life all alone? I don't mean the "I am single and never going to meet anyone, my life is over" kind of alone. If that's your attitude, you probably need to be slapped back into reality. Check your life, girl! Or boy. Get it together, people!

We aren't whining about our life because we don't have someone with us. NO ONE is attracted to someone who is

25

complaining all the time. Think of it as being "hard to get" and that confidence will get. you. noticed.

We all desire purpose...to truly understand that there is a reason why we exist. We desire connection. To find others in the world who get us and make us better people in the process. And we need to know that no matter what we have gone through in life, we still matter.

They (whoever they is) say that the average lifespan is approximately 78 years. That is roughly 28,489 days here on earth (yes, I used a calculator). In the grand scheme of things, that is not a lot of time. Life begins and life ends every day. New generations rise up and take the place of the old ones. Some of us will live longer than 78 years and yet some of us will have a much shorter time here.

Our time then becomes very valuable, almost fragile.

## LEARN FROM YOUR ELDERS

I love to sit and listen to my grandparents tell stories. They have such fascinating narrations and possess such great wisdom.

Life was so different then, and I will be the first to say that I probably would not have survived. I like my technology. I really like my Netflix. And I love my Keurig! But I am always in awe of how life was for my Mamaws and Papaws as they grew up.

And even with our differences, they have influenced my

life. Their lives play a major part in how my life is lived today.

They know the true definition of hard work, and I know most of us today do not understand that concept. I haven't worked in a factory during the war and I haven't risen with the sun to plow fields. The power of determination and pushing through no matter what obstacles occur is something they SURVIVED.

The Depression was tragic and beyond hard, yet they sacrificed and persevered, which in turn affected my parents, which in turn allowed me to be the generation that works from my computer at Starbucks and sips green tea at Panera. This legacy of hard work gives me confidence and a strong belief in what I can pursue despite the challenges that come.

This is the ripple effect.

Their foundations of hard work, sacrifice, and faith in God remind me of what is important. To remember that much of life is determined by what you are ready to put into it. And they have each lived exceptional lives because they put in the work.

The question becomes, "What do we do with the time we are given? Do we let life pass us by or do we realize that we are each here for a reason?"

Although we may not all make the cover of a magazine, there is still the need to live the type of life that will continue to make a difference even after we are gone.

We need to understand the *why* of our lives.

This is where it gets really good folks!

If I could, I would get right in your face and make sure you hear me. This stuff gets me excited!

## THE WHY OF OUR LIVES...AND MORE QUESTIONS

In the end, will we look back and regret how we spent our limited number of days on this earth or will we know that we did our part to live a meaningful life with whatever time we were given?

Are we able to make an impact that will reach farther than our meager time on earth?

Future impacts aside, will we live today in such a way as to feel fulfilled and purpose driven?

I believe that inside each of us is a need for validation and purpose. We want others to know that we exist and that we are not just here to take up space.

Knowing why we are here helps us to make the most with the time we are given. Knowing how that *why* fits into the story of the world will take our lives to a completely new level.

That three letter word is the reason for this book. It is one thing to know the dream for your life, but we must grasp why we should live it out. There are others who depend on us to live out our dreams. Think of the jobs that were created because Steve Jobs overcame adversity and started Apple. What would our cultural diversity in America have been without Martin Luther King, Jr.? Can you imagine not being able to reach your spouse or kids at a moment's notice? Thank you, Thomas Edison.

Great people who lived out their dreams became major players in shaping the ability for us to reach our own.

It is so good!

## I DARE YOU TO DREAM

Let's talk about dreams for just a minute.

As children, our dreams don't seem that far off. In fact, we believe in them so much that we don't wait to become adults. As kids, we instantly become a firefighter, a singer, a mom, a dancer, a doctor, a race car driver.

Or the next big superstar.

Yes, as a child I believed that I would be the next American Idol! Long before that show was ever thought of (and go on to have way too many seasons), I knew I would be the next Lionel Richie or Debbie Gibson. It was the 80's people!

Our backyard was my stage. I would strap my Walkman on my waist, pop in my favorite cassette tape, and perform my way to stardom complete with a popped collar, acid wash jeans, and tube socks with the stripes at the top.

I was what they call a triple threat—singer, dancer, and actor! I forced my sisters to join me in creating a band and made it mandatory to rehearse day-in and day-out. I then forced them to execute a flawless performance in front of an audience of two people. Yes, that would be mom and dad.

Don't judge me.

But it's true. As children, the line between our dreams and reality is so blurred that it almost does not even exist. Nothing holds us back. Children do not let fear stand in their way. They don't come up with a million reasons why they can't be something. They just are who they want to be.

Somewhere along the path of life, this changes. As adults, we let life deter us from staying the course. Chasing after our dreams slowly slips out of our grip.

We come up with a lot of excuses for it: getting older, paying bills, staying in a job we do not really like, getting married, having kids. The truth is they are just excuses and we allow ourselves to settle for an average life instead of truly living the life we were meant to live.

What if we chose a different way? What if decided that average was not the way for us? What if we chose to not be yet another person that looks back on their life and wonders "what if?"

What if I had...

—lived a better life?

—not taken my relationships for granted?

—lived out my dreams?

—set goals?

—done something about it rather than just talked about it?

—focused on having more fun in life?

—complained less?

—hustled more and made it happen?

What if we took another step back and were able to see our life from a broader perspective?

If we were able to connect the dots and see how our life plays a much bigger role in the way the world turns than we realize.

You see, I believe there is a much bigger reason why we were meant to live out our purpose in life. Yes, it creates a much more fulfilled life for us. Yes, it affects our mindset, our outlook, the way we carry ourselves. It changes the way we go to bed at night and why we wake up in the mornings.

But there is a much bigger reason. You see, it is not just about us.

There is a world out there that desperately needs us to live out our dreams, our goals, our purpose. They need us to work hard, to hustle, to succeed, to even fail, but to not give up. Because the way we live out our lives does not only affect us. It affects our family, our friends, our neighbors, and our coworkers. It affects people at our church, those we go to school with, those

> # Are we able to make an impact that will reach farther than our meager time on earth?

we see on a daily basis and those we simply meet once in our lifetime.

It even affects those we will never even meet.

When I discovered this truth, it was a breakthrough moment for me! I had thought many times about the people that had inspired me to live out my dreams because they were living out theirs. Seeing people do what they love, accomplish goals, and strive for better lives motivated me to do the same. It energized me!

But then I realized that I was meant to keep that momentum going. By desiring more with my own life and actually doing it, I would encourage others to do the same. It's this beautiful idea of how we as humans are much more connected than we realize. We were meant to work together. We were meant to hustle.

In fact, you can hustle at your hustle. It's both a verb *and* a noun! Your dream, goal, passion, or pursuit is the hustle that the world needs. You can inspire someone with your activity.

Looking at our goals and dreams this way also broadens our view of how our own lives work. When we remember that our lives affect others, it takes our own dreams and goals to a new level. It deepens our motivation to get it done. It expands our why.

Our dreams take work. It takes hustle on our part. We cannot give up because the world needs us. No matter what your dream is for your life, I promise that it is much bigger than you realize. And if you could take a step outside of yourself, you would see it. If we all could broaden our scope on life, we would see how we are all connected.

That is what this book is about.

I believe that our lives are meant for so much more than just our own self-fulfillment. Just as our lives were forever impacted because of how someone else lived their life; so will we impact others by the way we live ours.

It is more important than we realize.

This is where it gets intoxicating! Once you are able to start living the fullest expression of your own life, you start understanding how it plays a part in the rest of the world. It takes on a deeper meaning. It takes on a more impactful meaning. You begin to see the world in a new way!

As you read this book, my hope is that you are able to grasp that truth and allow it to change you.

There is a world out there that needs us to keep living, to keep dreaming, to keep hustling. They need to know that we are giving it our best shot because they are worth living for. We know that life is not easy and that our goals and dreams will take a lot of work, but when we understand the why, when we grasp the depth of the impact our lives can make, we must continue.

That is why I wrote this book. That is why you are reading this book. That is why the opening sentence got you to here. It is all meant for a reason.

The world needs your hustle.

# WRITE IT DOWN:

What is the dream for your life?

_____

_____

_____

_____

_____

_____

As a child what did you want to be when you grew up?

_____

_____

_____

_____

_____

_____

# WRITE IT DOWN:

Are you happy with where your life is right now?

_____

_____

_____

_____

_____

_____

_____

What changes do you desire in your life?

_____

_____

_____

_____

_____

_____

# DEFINING YOUR HUSTLE

*The world needs your hustle.*
*It needs your dreams,*
*your goals, your vision.*

Your life matters.

Let's stop right there for a minute.

Yes, three words in and I'm telling you to stop. Those three words hold such power and freedom. Fifteen letters that are vital to the message of this book.

Before you can impact others, you need to believe what those words say. Read it again. I dare you to say it out loud.

Your. Life. Matters.

Did you say it? Do you *believe* it?

Are these empty words that simply fall on deaf ears, or do they breathe life into your soul? I believe that no matter where you are in your journey, no matter what your circumstances are, no matter what you have done or what you want to do, your life truly matters.

Think about it. You did not show up here by chance. You were created, and that means you matter. The One who created you is full of perfection and grace, imparting life to each breath you take. You are not a mistake. You add beauty, meaning, and all kinds of awesome to this world.

Your life matters.

When this truth began to permeate my life, it added so much depth, purpose, and motivation to what I was doing. We all struggle with doubt, and there are days when we feel as though we are simply taking up space. Those lies could not be farther from the truth.

Our strengths, imperfections, passions, faults...it all matters.

You must grasp this truth in order to truly live out your dreams. Maybe you need to write it on a note card and tape it to the mirror. Maybe you need to say it out loud every morning. Whatever it takes to let this truth become a part of who you are.

Once you do, you will begin to understand that your dreams and goals are there for a reason. If our lives matter, then what we are meant to do with them definitely matters! We were created with unique strengths, talents, abilities, and passions. As cheesy and cliché as it sounds, it is true that only you can do what you were meant to do. No one else can!

God knew what He was doing–the place you were born, the specific moment in the time spectrum, the family you were given reveals intentional thought. Every little detail played a role in shaping who you would become from the beginning.

I realize that for some of you this is hard to believe. Maybe your childhood was anything but ideal, you had a horrible relationship with your parents, you grew up in a dreadful environment, or there are things in your past you never want to revisit. I hope that as you work through your past, you will see that it can still be used for good. It shapes who you are today and gives you strength to change the cycle for future generations. It allows you to connect with others of similar backgrounds and help them to find their way to a better life.

No matter how our life came to be, it plays a part in

how we fit into the world. Our personalities, our talents, and our passions were woven together to create our gifts that we must share with the world.

MUST.

Not gifts we *might* need to share. Not gifts that we *probably* should tell someone about on a good day. Nope!

I am talking about gifts that we must share with the world!

This is good stuff, people, as in "climb-to-the-top-of-a-mountain-and-sing-from-the-top-of-your-lungs" kind of good stuff! It's not a question of if you were given a gift. We all were. It's a matter of understanding what that gift is and how it can be fully expressed in your life.

> # No matter where you are in your journey, no matter what your circumstances are, no matter what you have done or what you want to do, your life truly matters.

What is your dream?

Lauren Athalia knew early on that photography was in her genes. As a child, she saw life in moments she didn't want to forget. The people, the places, and experiences were all something she wanted to capture and hold in her hands. The problem was that she didn't know how to channel her passion.

When she was fourteen, she borrowed her mom's broken point-and-shoot camera. That changed everything.

Finally, she had a way to stop time. She could capture what she saw in her head and make it tangible. This fueled her passion and for the next few years she fell in love with taking photographs. She realized that her passion was also directly connected with her purpose in life. This began a stirring inside to see how her photography could make a difference in the lives of others.

This is key. Our passions and purpose are always meant to work together. They are never supposed to clash or cause conflict. Also, our purpose should always include the question of how it will serve others. Our goals and dreams are never meant for only us. We should always tie our purpose in with the ability to serve.

Lauren knew she loved to capture and create moments. She also knew others wanted to do the same with moments in their life but did not have the talent or ability to do it with the artistic flare she could. This ability to meet the needs of others was her way to grow her passion into a business. It was also her opportunity to connect with her clients and learn their story. This added depth and meaning to what she was doing.

Lauren hustled and now instead of capturing moments with that broken point-and-shoot camera, she has had the chance to photograph celebrities and international corporate clients. Her work has gained national attention and her passion has grown to a new level!

Life showed Lauren her passion early on. She didn't dismiss it. She found a way for her passion to thrive. She knew her life mattered and that she was meant to make a difference in the lives of others. And now she is capturing beautiful moments for other people to have forever.

Once you begin to live in the truth that your life matters, your dreams and goals really come alive. This book obviously talks about the word hustle a lot, but the truth is— before you can hustle, you have to know what your hustle actually is.

You have to define your dream or your goal. Without it, you are simply running around like a crazy person with no direction. Who wants to be that person?

## YOUR HUSTLE IS NATURAL

I lead a #5AMClub online. It is a group comprised of people who get up at 5:00 AM to work on their hustles. What's that, you say? You didn't know there was such a thing as 5:00 AM? Oh yes, my friend, there is. And it is glorious! I highly recommend experiencing it!

It's not enough to get up at 5 AM and stare at the clock. Without a purpose or "why," you're just the person sitting at the table with bed head, with no clue as to how you got there or why you are still sitting there. Not cute, people. Not cute at all.

I am a morning person and do my best work early in the mornings. The reason it works for me is because I have a specific reason for why I get up. That, and I drink dark, extra bold, kick you in the face kind of coffee as soon as I wake up. That helps, too.

I love the early mornings now. I do a lot of my blogging at 5:00 AM. In fact, most of this book was written in the wee morning hours. Besides the coffee turning me into the Energizer Bunny, it was my reason to get up.

My insanely talented and hilarious friend Bethany Jett, who is *totally trying* to be a morning person, told me her trick for getting things done. At night, she plans out a few things that have to be accomplished the next day. She's in "boss mode." The next morning, she puts on her "employee" hat and works to get the job done. Great advice!

Some mornings, I even jump out of bed because I cannot wait to get started! Admittedly, there are some mornings when I stumble down to the dining room table, pry my eyes open, and have to waterboard myself in order to get my body going!

When people tell me they find it extremely hard to get up so early, and that they lack the motivation to follow-through, I normally ask them about their "why" first.

*Why* are you getting up so early?

The same can be said for hustling. In order for the rest

of this book to make sense, you need to determine what it is you want to accomplish. What is your goal? What is your dream? And then why. Once you figure that out, the rest begins to fall into place.

*Write your why:*

_____

_____

_____

I can see it now. Some of you filled in your why with gusto. Some of you left those lines blank because you hate writing in books, but some of you honestly don't really know what your dream is, much less why.

That's okay.

If you find yourself saying, "Kevin, I don't know my purpose. If it's Netflix binging, then yes, I know exactly what my purpose is. But besides that, I got nothing."

I say again, it's okay.

Although Netflix binging would be an awesome job to have, I think you might be meant for more. And yes, I have taken on the title of Professional Netflix Binger a few weekends of my life. We all have. With shows like *Breaking Bad*, *The Walking Dead*, and *The Unbreakable Kimmy Schmidt*, how can you not?

Fortunately, discovering our purpose and dreams might be easier than we think. I believe life is constantly showing us what our purpose is. However, I know how frustrating it can be to hear people talk on and on about their purpose with such grandiose terms, and meanwhile we are just over here on the couch watching *The Kardashians* and eating bon-bons.

It's weird that I chose "bon-bons" because I don't believe I have ever actually had one. However, I have been keeping up with that Kardashian clan for quite some time.

When it comes to our purpose, I think many times we make it harder than it has to be. We are waiting for some big Hallelujah moment in the sky, and that

> **I believe life is constantly showing us what our purpose is.**

is not always going to happen. We simply need to look at our life and see that it is revealing what we are meant to do,

It is more about paying attention and seeing what is right in front of us.

As a child, I was always a dreamer. I grew up watching *Kids Incorporated* and the *All New Mickey Mouse Club*, the one where Justin Timberlake and Britney Spears got their start. It featured video Tuesdays where they produced their own music videos to current songs at the time. If you know what I am talking about, we are instant friends. If you know the band, "The Party" that came out of the *All New Mickey Mouse Club*, we are instant besties!

But back to the story.

As a child, I knew I wanted to do big things with my life. It is how I have always been wired. As a child, I did not only dream about those things, I actually did them! In church, I was always the lead in every musical and play. I forced my sisters and neighbors to participate in original, Oscar-worthy plays and shows I wrote as a kid. My parents sat through more living room performances than they probably cared for, but I loved that creative side of life.

This continued on through my high school and college years. I was a worship leader at my church. I had my own worship band that traveled during the summers playing at various youth camps and retreats, which are not as glamorous as it sounds.

By "traveling band," I mean five guys in an extended pickup truck with a trailer hooked to the back. We stayed in primitive locations and played for what I would later learn to be extremely skimpy paychecks. But I still enjoyed every minute of it. I knew in those moments that I was doing what I was created to do.

As a kid, I enjoyed the performance side of things (#superstar), and as I grew older, I really enjoyed being able to use that platform to encourage people and make a difference. I found the meaning behind that natural ability of being in front of people–the ability to connect with people.

You have a similar story. What made you feel alive when you were a kid? What would you do every single day if money were no option? Who have you forced to read, watch, or listen to something that you've created? That's the crux of your purpose.

If I had to draw pictures every day of my life, I would die, but Scott Cuzzo is fulfilling a passion by creating adult coloring books. If people depended on me for any type of tech support, I'd be fired in a heartbeat; however, Jim Bob Howard is the man when it comes to all things computer related.

The natural talents and gifts are where we achieve our best results and feel fulfilled while doing them, even if our paychecks don't always reflect our skills. While we want to earn an amazing living using our gifts, the point is that I would write and coach for free if money were no option, and will use my time to develop these skills as I grow into my God-given roles.

## PURPOSE IS PLURAL

Please don't get so caught up in thinking you can only have one purpose. That kind of pressure will stress you out. No, you can have many. Your purpose contains many gifts that work together. So technically, purpose is singular, but we're gonna say it's plural. You are created to do many things. Don't put yourself into that proverbial box. Unless you're a mime. Then you can stay in one.

Most of us have a broad, larger theme to our lives, a

bigger purpose of why we were created. But underneath that are many ways to live that out and many avenues to take. It can change throughout our lives and that's okay.

My life expressed itself in many ways through the years, but it always fit under the category of encouraging others to know that their life matters, to believe in their goals and dreams, and to understand why they should live it out now.

## CATEGORIES

What's your category? If you're having trouble picking a path, let's find some commonalities.

Take a few minutes and look back over your life and list the things you were good at as a child, teen, young adult, and adult. What did you dream about? What games did you play as a child? What experiences brought out that child-like excitement we all long to capture again as adults? As you process, some common elements should appear.

Chances are, some of your childhood experiences were meant to show you the direction your life needs to go.

Did you love to build and design things as a child? Were you the one who expressed maternal instincts even at a young age? Were you fascinated more than most with science and how things work? Maybe your neighbors were impressed with your ability to not only create an award-winning lemonade stand but also your ability to persuade every single passer-by that drove by to stop and buy multiple cups!

Rest assured, if your goals and dreams include changes, that's okay. In fact, it's probably great news because it means you are growing and discovering your best strengths. Whew! Do you feel better about that? I know I do.

If you are struggling with knowing what to do with your life, I would encourage you to write down memories you had as a child and identify any common themes.

For some of you, childhood is not something you like to think about. It was a tough time in your life. You may not have had the ideal childhood, but you still dreamt of what you wanted to be when you grew up. I believe we are all born with that desire. Always remember the good memories of what you wanted to be as a child.

Our purpose begins to reveal itself to us early on and confirms the truth that we need to live out our best lives. The answer has been there all along. We have been equipped since day one. It's right there. Your

> **The answer has been there all along. We have been equipped since day one.**

purpose might need some help expressing itself, but rest assured, you already have what it takes.

For so many of us, the disconnect happens when we enter adulthood and get stuck in a job that we really did not want. I mean, who really wants to grow up and be the person who cleans the porta potty? It's a crappy job, but someone's got to do it. Those guys should be earning six-figures because we need them.

If you find yourself stuck in a job that isn't fulfilling your purpose, get out! Life happens, and we lose the dreams and child-like belief that is vital to our lives. We grow up and start to follow a path that was previously paved for us by society. They said, "This is how it should be!", and we blindly followed. Slowly, the dreams we once believed in got lost in the masquerade of what life was supposed to look like.

It can be hard to remove the mask and see what has been waiting underneath, but the good news is that it can be done. The dreams and goals in our life can still be redeemed, and many times, that comes from going back to the beginning.

I encourage you to revisit that part of yourself that has been pushed back. There is a reason you were given those interests, strengths and unique traits. Yes, life does happen. Relationships, kids, jobs, bills, circumstances - they all happen. But it never meant that we had to lose ourselves in the process.

So do you have it? Do you have that dream or goal in mind? If not, it's OK. It will come to you. And if you do know your dream and your *why*, then we are about to give it depth and meaning and make it bigger than you realized!

I feel like we should high five or hug or something! Maybe throw glitter in the air!

# WRITE IT DOWN:

Write "my life matters" on a card and tape it to your mirror for one week.

_____

_____

_____

_____

What do you believe is the dream for your life?

_____

_____

_____

_____

What is one goal you want to accomplish in the next thirty days.

_____

_____

_____

_____

# YOU GET A GIFT!
# YOU GET A GIFT!
# EVERYBODY GETS A GIFT!

*It needs the gift you have been given,*
*unique and meant to be expressed.*

In 2011, Sarah Harmeyer held a position at a children's hospital. Work was her life and her life was work.

Eventually, she felt like God was telling her to step back, take some time, and figure out who she really was. So Sarah did just that. She met with a trusted friend and they talked every week for three months. She began to rediscover herself and her identity in who God said she was, not in what she did.

By paying attention to what made her come alive, she realized that what she loved most was being a people-gatherer and found value through the connections that were made if she created an environment for them to happen. When she hosted dinner parties, her guests commented repeatedly that it was the best dinner party they had ever been to, confirming her gifts.

Life was showing her what she was meant to do. Once we define our hustle, we need to believe in it. We need to realize there truly is something inside each of us that is meant to be shared. It is what makes us unique and can be expressed in a myriad of ways.

For some, that gift may be music. You have a gift of singing or playing an instrument. It adds beauty, emotion, and connection. That needs to be shared with the world! We need your gift! *Unless you are one of those first round American Idol auditions that gets sent home because well, you really cannot sing. Seriously, the world does not need that mess. Next!*

Maybe your gift is parenting—one of the most important

yet under-appreciated gifts in the history of the human race. You are raising, teaching, and shaping the lives of little human beings! That is crazy important!

Although I am not a parent, I have seen it done right and I have seen it done wrong. And oh, does it make a difference! We need your gift! We need you to believe there is purpose and meaning and so much importance in what you are doing, even on the days you want to pull your hair out because those precious little ones are about to drive you bleeping crazy!

Your gift is unique. Sure it may be similar to what someone else is doing but what makes it unique is that it comes from you. Your personality, your perspective, your strength—it's your personal touch that no else can fully replicate.

Maybe your gift is building a table, placing it in your backyard, and inviting others over for a meal that is centered around intention, community, and love

In 2012, Sarah decided to expand her idea of being a people-gatherer. She asked her father if he would build her a table that was big enough to seat twenty people. He built an 18-foot, farmhouse-style table and she put it in her backyard. She then set a goal to seat five hundred people around that table, hosting one dinner after another, within a year's time.

By Thanksgiving of that year, the 500th person showed up. Her dream became a reality. She visualized what truly made her feel alive. Growth came from her obedience.

Then it was time to expand that vision. That 18-foot table wasn't meant to be the only one. She realized other people might want to do the same so she and her dad built more tables.

She decided to call her new project Neighbor's Table, with an intentional apostrophe because the table belongs to the neighbors. The tagline: *A Love Mission.*

Sarah genuinely loves people and that love of others was meant to be involved in the purpose of her life. Her new goal is to have a Neighbor's Table in all 50 states by the year 2020.

Sarah said yes to her dream. She said yes to the idea of Neighbor's Table. Because of that yes, it is no longer an idea, but a reality. Sarah would be the first to say that it has not always been easy. There have been fears and obstacles along the way, but she continued. She didn't give up and her tables are bringing people together and fulfilling her mission of love.

I had the opportunity to attend a Neighbor's Table event once and it was an experience I will never forget. Sarah is extremely intentional about the purpose of the evening and it shows in every detail. It was a beautiful moment as I sat at this elegantly dressed table and learned the stories of others around me.

I love Sarah's story for many reasons. Her gift in life is loving people. That gift is expressed in the ability to gather people together. Life was showing her all along how she can use it to make a difference in the lives of others. That gift was just waiting to be released.

I hope Sarah's story inspires you to say yes to your dreams. There are countless stories of those who found their passion and turned it into something that impacted others in ways they never would have thought possible.

I believe that our gifts are waiting to be released because I believe that it has been a part of us since the day we were born. It is part of how we were created and designed. The more I have thought about that idea, the more it has given me confidence to live out my purpose.

Sometimes we spend so much time searching for what has been there all along.

We all struggle with doubt and insecurity, especially when it comes to our goals and dreams. We can think of a thousand reasons why we aren't qualified to accomplish them. We believe that others can do it better. We don't think that we have what it takes. We feel like we are being too cocky if we think otherwise.

But if we were created to live out our dreams and accomplish goals, then wouldn't it make sense that we would be equipped to do so? Sure, we might need to educate ourselves to learn the skills. We might need to train in order to get better. We might have to say yes to things in order for those passions to emerge.

The idea that our dream was there all along should be a confidence booster. It's a beautiful thought, really. A lot of times, we only realize this in hindsight. We see how life was working all along to get us where we are. I want to encourage you to use this truth to help push past some of the fear.

Take the leap now knowing that you have what it takes to make it happen.

> ## We need to realize there truly is something inside each of us that is meant to be shared.

## CREATING TIME

Rachel Mayo is my best friend, the kind of friend you consider to be your soul mate in the realm of friendships. We always refer to ourselves as "twinsies that came from different parents." Oh, and we are ten years apart in age. She is the younger one. She would want you to know that.

Rachel is the creator of RachelBee Designs. She is crazy talented at hand-lettering. Rachel can bring words to life with such artistic beauty. I love that I can call her my best friend and that we support and encourage each other to make our dreams happen and to continually dream bigger.

Rachel's passion for lettering started as a teenager when she would doodle all over her notebooks. As many girls and boys do, she would doodle words and shapes and curly q's as a way to pass the time.

These doodles became something more.

Instead of being decorations on her pink Trapper Keeper®, she realized they could mean something to other people. It was a natural talent, a gift that was a part of who she was. Her unique gift was meant to be expressed to make a difference in the lives of others.

Now, she has taken doodling to a new level! She does hand-lettering for prints, cards, wedding invitations, boards, and even created an entire wall! Her gift visualizes words and makes them beautiful. It adds to the experience. She takes a simple word or phrase and makes it come alive. People notice. Her work has played a part in some of the best moments of her clients' lives.

Life showed Rachel early on what a dream in her life could be. Not only what it could be, but what it should be. It has taken a lot of hustle on her part. She currently works a full-time job and does RachelBee Designs on the side. That means lots of late nights, weekends, and any other hours she can find to put her hands to work.

I believe I can speak for Rachel in saying that it's not all fun and games. Those late hours get tiring at times. No matter how fun a project is, some days her hand cramps into a permanent Sharpie-holding position. However, the hustle is paying off. She is very close to turning her side business into a full-time career!

Rachel sees the vision. She knows the end result. She understands how her work makes a difference in people's lives. When she delivers the finished product, it can make a lasting impression. Does the world need her hustle? Oh yes!

One of the things I love about Rachel's story is that her gift wasn't hard to find. She didn't lay in bed at night wondering, "what the heck am I good at?" Her talent showed up early in her day-to-day life.

It was something she already loved to do.

She focused and began perfecting her craft. She realized how it could serve other people and decided to turn that into a business! That is a great lesson for us all. Don't make finding your dream harder than it needs to be. Most of the time life is showing it to us every day.

> # Growth comes from our obedience.

## IT'S TIME FOR PRO BONO

Too many times we want to wait until our gifts start making us money before we really hustle after them. You have probably heard the question—what would you do even if no one paid you for it? This is the time to put it into practice.

Use your talents and volunteer. There are plenty of organizations, groups, and companies who would love to have you volunteer a few hours a week. You have something they need and what better way to try out your ideas than with volunteering? You will see what it's really about and find out if it is something you should pursue or maybe step back and reconsider.

Also, networking is a must. Reach out to those who are already doing what you want to do and learn from them. See if you can help out in any kind of way. Go to events and talk to people. Networking can open doors and connect you with people who could help propel your goal or dream into a reality!

That's what Sarah did. She didn't start out building all these tables and trying to sell them. She began by inviting people over. Her mission wasn't to make money. It was to build community. She tried it out in her own backyard and from there, her passion thrived into what it is today.

The same is true with Rachel. She began by doodling things for people because they took notice in her talent. She has volunteered a lot of her work without ever making a dime. Why? Because she knows her passion connects with people.

Do you recognize your gift? If not, don't overcomplicate it. As we discussed earlier, think of the things you love to do. What were your passions early on? What are they now. Your life matters because you have something unique to offer the world. And without it, the world loses some of its beauty. Therefore, what you have to offer is meant to be expressed.

I don't believe God created us with gifts we are

supposed to keep to ourselves. Again it goes back to the idea that we are all more connected than we realize. Our lives and the gifts inside help to fill a void in someone else.

No one is perfect. We will never experience balance on our own. Our greatest strengths help carry someone else in their weakness. People come into our lives for a reason. They serve as a guide. So yes, our gifts are there for a reason.

Does your life have value? Is there something about you that others need? Yes! I cannot say yes enough! Yes! Yes! Yes! YES! Once you realize what that is and unlock its potential, you will begin to connect to the bigger picture of life and how it connects with others.

It is waiting. But it is up to you to make it happen.

# WRITE IT DOWN:

What are three of your greatest strengths, talents, or abilities?

_____

_____

_____

_____

_____

_____

Is there a passion, talent, or something you enjoy already in your life that you could do more with?

_____

_____

_____

_____

_____

_____

_____

# WRITE IT DOWN:

Are there people in your life who have taken a gift and turned it into something more?

_____

_____

_____

_____

_____

_____

Where could you volunteer and help curate your talents? Find an opportunity to serve within the next thirty days.

_____

_____

_____

_____

_____

# THE HUSTLE TRIFECTA

*The world needs your hustle.*
*It needs your ideas, your faith in the unknown,*
*your hope for a better life.*

I'm a dreamer. Always have been. I can come up with an idea every week. Sometimes every day. What I've learned (and others who have to listen to me) is that if I keep talking about an idea, it might be something worth pursuing. If I forget about it the next day, probably not. I have had plenty of both.

Like the time I told my sisters and our two best friends that we would be forming a band and become world famous rock stars! I was a teenager at the time, but I was confident that this was our life's dream. I had the vision for sure. I made them all practice for hours on end. The one thing I forgot was that there wasn't a lot of musical talent between the five of us. Not my best idea.

Or the time I had the genius idea that "Words on Rocks" would become the next big thing! You might remember a guy who started writing messages on potatoes and made thousands of dollars a month. Crazy, I know. So crazy that I thought, what if I wrote words on rocks and sold them? People would love that! I would be a millionaire! My rocks would be everywhere!

Well, I sold one order to someone out in California. I made $10! It didn't quite catch on like I thought it would. So yeah, really not a good idea. Thank you to the anonymous person in California who now owns rocks with words on them! They will be worth millions one day.

You might notice a common theme—my desire to be super famous and super rich. Basically, I'm the missing child from the Kardashian crew. I already have the "K" name and everything. Kim, Kourtney, Khloé, and Kevin. I'm ready and waiting!

We all have good ideas and are usually quite proud when all goes well. You might give yourself a little pat on the back and say, "job well done!" It is fun to be the person that comes up with a really good ideas. People applaud you. People admire you. People tend to like that guy!

But we also have ideas that make us say, "Oh wow! No, stop. Reverse. Delete! Ignore!" It is similar to those text messages we send in the heat of the moment. Sure in that moment we feel fully justified in what we are about to say to the recipient. They deserve to read these words, of which we mean every one of them! And as soon as we hit send, we feel ourselves in slow motion wanting to punch through the phone and grab that message before it goes out into the world.

We have all been there.

When it comes to our goals and dreams, we might have to try before we know whether or not we have a good idea. The day will come when we have to face failure in order to know if it was right or not. I believe that failure is meant to be there. Sure, it isn't fun to fall flat on our face, but if we are able to pick ourselves up and keep going, then the failure was not in vain.

Let's not make that too sweet sounding. The failure part is gonna suck! You will wish that you could go back in time and do it differently. People are going to give you the pity look. They will shake their heads in embarrassment for you. Under their breath, they will say how they saw it coming but it's precious that you tried.

Failure has a tendency to shake our confidence. That's the understatement of the year, right? If you're like me, you get a little bit dramatic and wonder what the hell you were thinking for even trying? I'm a nobody! I'm such a failure! Where is Ben & Jerry? It's a low point that isn't cute to watch.

It's what we choose to do with it that really makes a difference. Not succeeding does not mean you have to re-think your entire existence. It simply means you tried, it didn't work, you learn, and move on.

> **Not succeeding does not mean you have to re-think your entire existence. It simply means you tried, it didn't work, you learn, and move on.**

So, those ideas you have? Try them! Don't get caught up in what the end result will be that you allow fear to stop you from ever trying. How will you ever know what could be if you don't ever try?

Let me give some practical advice. Seek out friends or others whom you trust and share your ideas with them. See what kind of response they give you. Or try your idea on a smaller scale before launching it worldwide. There is nothing wrong with testing the waters. In fact, I would say it is a great idea to do just that. Feedback and suggestions from the right people can help you launch your hustles more successfully and effectively.

Will we have great ideas? Yes!

Will we have horrible ideas? Yes!

But ideas are what lead to better lives. Both the good and the bad ones. They help unlock our potential. They show us what we are capable of doing, and they provide outlets to live out our dreams and goals.

What idea has been swirling in your head for a while? What can you do today to start making it happen? A small step is better than no step at all. Write it out. Tell someone. Put action to your words. Start!


## FAITH IN THE UNKNOWN

Living your dream requires the ability to have faith in the unknown. Many times we can see the end result in our minds. We know what we want, but we don't know how we will get there.

The unknown is such a great place to be, right? It gives us such a warm and cozy feeling, like being tickled by the tail of a unicorn.

Umm, no Kevin. That's not it at all! It is more like being blindfolded in a forest and told to find your way back to civilization. You have no idea where to go, your arms are flailing around, and you might scream. Like a little girl.

Basically, it can be scary as hell.

But I cannot stop right there. If I did, you'd probably go dumpster diving for that receipt! Let's try to find some hope. Yes, the unknown is a certainty. It's going to happen. It's part of life. But faith is what carries us through to the finish line. When you can believe in what you are doing, and know that your dream was given to you for a reason, that belief will carry you through those dark and scary moments.

And if all else fails, go to your happy place.

Faith is a strong component in turning your wants and desires that live in your head into the reality of your life. The truth is, not everyone is going to support you. You won't always have the applause and encouragement of others.

And that's okay .

My good friend, Matt Ham, wrote a much needed article for his blog MattHam.com that talked about how many times our family and closest friends will not show the amount of support that we expect from them. It may not make sense to us, but they might not be our audience. And when you don't have that, do you give up or do you keep going?

In his article, "What Breakfast with my Best Friend Taught me about my Success as a Writer," Matt shares the story of how his best friend Jake spoke honest truth into his life when Matt voiced his concern for Jake's lack of support.

What I read knocked me over because so many of us can relate. It's all about losing the right perspective on our dreams. Here is an excerpt from that article.

As I lock myself away in my writing room, punching keys in an attempt to bring life to the ideas running circles through my head, I'm plagued by the ever-present question: Why are so many of my closest friends apathetic toward my dream?

In a social media environment where Facebook "likes" and Twitter retweets are as addictive as crack-cocaine, there's a constant battle to determine our success from the acceptance of others. And the acceptance of those who know us best seems to matter the most.

Although my blog just crossed 100,000 readers and my book has sold more than 1,500 copies, my best friend Jake hadn't subscribed to my site or even purchased a copy of *Redefine Rich*.

Deep down, in the places I refused to write about, that hurt.

As the pain grew, it gave way to fear. I started thinking about all of the friends—high school teammates, college buddies, work associates—who hadn't seemed to care about this new passion of mine. Fear lead to doubt, and doubt to insecurity.

Maybe I shouldn't be writing after all.

Maybe my dream isn't that important anyway.

Those voices sound silly, but that's the loudest crap we tend to listen to, isn't it?

I told Jake that one of the hardest things for me was wondering what he thought.

I told him I'd recently read that success is "striving so

that those who know you the best respect you the most." And according to that definition, I didn't feel very successful as a writer—to which he replied, "That just somebody's opinion, dude."

He then looked straight at me and said these words:

"You clearly have an audience because your stuff is doing great. But that's not why you began writing. You began writing because it was something you felt like you had to do. You're clearly helping people, but don't think that everyone is in your audience. Quit trying to please me. Focus on what your audience wants and give them more of that."

He was right.

Jake reminded me that success isn't always measured by the approval of those who are closest to us. Success is measured by our willingness to hold true to our deep conviction and pour everything we have into it, regardless of what everyone else says.

Bam! Those words were a much needed wakeup call for me! Stop thinking you are so great that everyone wants to be in your fan club. Your audience does not include everyone on this earth.

I can see how it seems that those closest to us should be extra excited for us. They should support us, encourage us, and throw all their money our way. But the truth is, they might not be our audience. Sure they are happy for us, but they might not connect with what we are doing the way others do.

And as Matt says, that's okay.

Once you start living your dream for the praise of others, you lose sight of why you started in the first place. It will lead you down a road that is an exhausting chase of burnout, unfulfilled flattery, and a circle of dead ends.

More importantly, it paves the way for doubt to enter into your life. Doubt works as a distraction to living out accomplished goals and dreams. It wants to keep you questioning your abilities, your choices, and the path you have taken. Doubt can be a strong deterrent in our lives if we allow it.

Or we can choose to overcome doubt with faith.

> # Stop thinking you are so great that everyone wants to be in your fan club. Your audience does not include everyone on this earth.

Faith is the motivation that moves you past the doubt. It hangs on when we start to lose our grip. It is the inner strength we desperately need to help keep our eyes on the prize when doubt and fear want to make our eyes wander from the truth of who we are.

Life will always include an unknown. No matter how hard we try, we can never know with confidence how things will turn out. But when you think about it, isn't that one of the exciting things about life? We don't know what is to come. It is an adventure that requires risk, courage, and a determination to keep going.

## EMBRACE THE UNKNOWN

Learn to embrace the unknown. Remember that you don't have to have it all figured out. Keep the faith that your dreams are being expressed in your life. As you continue, the unknown will lead you to some pretty cool places.

I love the last few words of this line from the poem - *your hope for a better life.* I think we all want that. We want something better because we know it's out there. We desire something more because we know it's possible.

And just as faith helps guide us to that place, hope is the power that pulls us out of ordinary and takes us to extraordinary. Hope lets us know that the life we are meant to live is possible. Our goals and dreams lead us to the better life we desire.

Hope is such a powerful force. It's a perspective changing word. It comes from deep within and can lead us out of the worst of circumstances. Maybe you have a good life but you want something better. Maybe you made some bad decisions that affected your life and now you want to make a change. Maybe you grew up in a home that was anything but loving and you are determined to break that cycle.

Whatever your reason for a better life, let hope guide you.

And do not be afraid to desire a better life. I am not sure why or how so many of us fell into this trap, but we have convinced ourselves that a better life cannot happen for us. We almost feel guilty for wanting a better way. Sure, other people can, but not me. We tell others they deserve it! But we end up settling for average or even less than average and do not allow ourselves to dream about anything other than what is right in front of us.

Why?

Why do others deserve it and you do not? Who fed you a lie that you have convinced yourself is the truth? It's as if we stand at the edge of a precipice and see a life out there waiting for us, yet we turn back without ever taking one step forward.

If this is you, please listen to me. Look me in the eye. Hear what I am about to say.

You deserve it! Your life matters! You are meant for more! The idea that you can't is a lie. Your hope for a better life is as worthy as the next person's.

Yes, for some it might mean more work. It might require breaking a cycle of average that has gone on for too long. And it will probably mean telling those who have played a part in instilling this lie to you to shut the hell up.

I would be more than happy to tell them for you. As long as they are not really big, strong, scary people. In that case, I will tell them from a distance… with a megaphone. And then run like crazy!

But yes, my friend. You have a hope for a better life, so give yourself permission to make it happen! Please do not get to the end of your life wishing you had tried. We get one shot at life and your life is so worth living.

> # Hope is the power that pull us out of ordinary and takes us to extraordinary.

What is the bigger reason we should believe in our hope for a better life? Because the world needs to know that it's okay for them to believe as well. If they see others create a better life for themselves, it might give them the motivation they need to take that first step towards their better life.

Remember that we are more connected than we realize. Our ability to live out a better life affects others taking the opportunity to do so as well.

The world needs to know that your ideas, your faith, and your hope is all there because it will affect their ability to say yes to the life they deserve. They will see your faith. They will be inspired by your hope. They will know that your ideas are changing the world.

# WRITE IT DOWN:

Write down 3 ideas you have when it comes to goals and dreams in your life. Don't worry about whether they or good or bad. You can figure that out later. This is a time to brainstorm!

_____

_____

_____

_____

_____

_____

What factors are keeping you from living the life you were meant to live?

_____

_____

_____

_____

_____

_____

# WRITE IT DOWN:

What things in your life give you hope now?

_____

_____

_____

_____

_____

_____

_____

_____

_____

_____

_____

_____

_____

_____

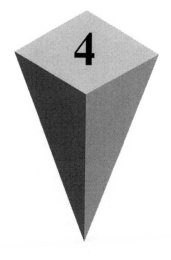

# THE NAKED TRUTH

*It needs you to be YOU.*
*My friend, your hustle matters*
*because the world matters.*

I don't know about you, but I am so turned off by the fakes of the world. You can usually see it coming from a mile away. FAKER! PHONY! SCAM!

In a world that screams at us on a daily basis with messages telling us how we should look and act and feel, we have become a people who will conform to whatever is the trend of the day.

Then next week, the trend changes and we spend all of our time trying to keep up the right appearance. Keeping up with the Joneses - whoever they are. It can really be exhausting. We keep chasing after an image we will never attain. And why is this?

Because we were never meant to be that person.

All the frustrations, all the worry, the never-ending search for satisfaction–they will always be there because the mirage will continually stay just out of our grasp.

We see this trait start early in life. As kids and teenagers, we want to be like the cool kids—the ones who stand out, the popular ones, the ones who dress well, have money, and just have that swagger. We want to be like them because society tells us to pursue that lifestyle.

I was never one of the cool kids.

I probably stood out for my sense of style, but it was not because it was "cool." I was friends with some of the popular kids in high school, but I should probably use that term loosely. I stood close to them at school functions rocking my hot pink polo, black vest and overly-large glasses.

And of course, the tight-rolled jeans were a must! Adding to the ensemble was a neon green and black hat I used to wear thinking it was cool. It was not. It was definitely not cool.

Maybe you didn't want to be one of the popular kids. Maybe you were in the nerd group (my glasses should have put me in that group), the scary gothic kids we used to pray for in Bible club, the Polo-wearing preppy kids who popped their collars with confidence, or any number of groups which form during those important high school years.

> **In a world that screams at us on a daily basis with messages telling us how we should look and act and feel, we have become a people who will conform to whatever is the trend of the day.**

Very few of us simply wanted to be ourselves.

It's hard to be the real deal when everyone is telling you to be someone else. We try this and that, anything and everything to fit in.

So what's the point? What kind of message are we sending when we are too afraid to be ourselves? What are we really afraid of?

We need more people who will live authentic lives.

# THE AUTHENTIC LIFE

Authenticity is one of my favorite words and something which took me years to learn. I have not perfected it, but I have learned to love who I was created to be, not who others wanted me to be.

Isn't it easier to simply be yourself? There is freedom in knowing who you are and not having to put up a front. Knowing all the quirks, the differences, the strengths—it is all a part of who you are and is there for a reason.

Learn to love the person you are...the person you are becoming...the person you were created to be. No matter what others tell you, you are beautiful just the way you are. There is a scripture verse, Psalms 139:14, which says, "I will praise You because I am fearfully and wonderfully made." This is the truth.

The problem seems to start early. Habits learned as children can often be the hardest to break. We are often taught to behave a certain way, act in a way that blends in more rather than stands out. There are certain expectations placed upon us based on gender, class, religion, or race.

In turn, unhealthy expectations make it harder and harder not only to be authentic but to find our true selves. It gets buried in years of being told what your life should look like.

Your originality is shrouded in family and friends who try to gain a second chance at life by living through yours. Their influence can be good, and at times we need guidance from others, yet we need to embrace the freedom to explore and understand who we truly are.

You were created. This means you matter. God did not form you to be a mold of anyone other than yourself. We do not need you to be the next anyone. We need you to be you.

Whether you realize it or not, you have something to offer.

As I have grown older, one thing that has made the biggest difference in my life is the ability to be exactly who I was created to be. I embrace what makes me unique, I'm comfortable in my own skin, and I try not to be anyone else but myself. I find that I am most drawn to those types of

> **The world needs real. They need authentic. They need vulnerable. They need flawed. They need you!**

people who know themselves and are not afraid to live that out.

This is what the world needs!

They need real. They need authentic. They need vulnerable. They need flawed. They need you!

And guess what? As I have learned to do more of this, I have connected with people on a much deeper level. As I share my struggles and flaws, there are some who say, "Yes! I have made the same mistakes." Or others who have said,

"Thank you for sharing your struggles." This doesn't mean we have to share every one of our deepest, darkest secrets with every stranger which comes our way. That would make for some very awkward moments. In fact, I should probably urge some of you not to do that.

But it frees us up from trying to be someone we are not. It allows us to be real in a world that tries to convince us every day to be what they want us to be.

Being authentic does not mean it will always be easy. Sometimes others do not want us to be ourselves. They get uncomfortable. It does not always fit the mold. At the end of the day, what is more important? That others are comfortable and happy, or that you were able to be yourself?

The world needs authenticity. It needs variety. It needs people of different races, religions, countries, and backgrounds to share their lives. In doing so, our differences create a beautiful picture of how the world works.

One of the exciting things about authenticity is how it directly relates to your goals and dreams. As you begin to understand who it is you were created to be, those dreams and goals will begin to surface as well. When this happens, life will begin to evolve into something much bigger than you thought possible.

You will realize how much your hustle really matters. Not only does it help bring about the fullest expression of yourself, but it plays a part in someone else fulfilling their dreams and goals.

## EMBRACE OTHERS

I speak from experience when I say it does not matter what others think. I have wasted time trying to be what others wanted and it never led to fulfillment. People connect with authenticity. They want to see you. Anyone who tries to suppress this has their own issues. We will let them deal with their own issues on someone else's couch! Am I right?

And as a side note—if you want others to embrace your authenticity, be sure you are doing the same for them. Celebrate your friends' differences. Take the time to learn your co-workers' stories. Before you write someone off because they aren't like you, remember that their life matters just as much as yours.

Our lives were never meant to be lived only for ourselves. We are connected with others in ways much bigger than we can possibly fathom. One of the tangible ways we know that we matter is how others impact us. They invest in us. They acknowledge our existence.

This is the point where our hustle takes on a much deeper meaning. You see, as we fulfill our purpose, it affects someone else fulfilling theirs. There are others out there who are counting on us to live the best lives we can. Whether it is our family or friends who are impacted over time, or a chance encounter with a stranger that alters their path, we are continually impacting others.

When moments come which cause us to question why we should keep hustling...

When we wonder if all of this hard work is worth it...

When it is much easier to give up, remember the people who are counting on you.

Remember that there are people who will find the courage to start their journey because you have continued on in yours.

They will know their goals and dreams matter because your life told them it did. Whatever it is their life is meant to accomplish, it will matter. It will fit into the bigger picture of the world and adds to the beauty of how this all works.

# WRITE IT DOWN:

What are five characteristics you love about yourself.

_____

_____

_____

_____

_____

_____

What parts of your childhood have you lost and would like to regain?

_____

_____

_____

_____

_____

_____

# WRITE IT DOWN:

If someone saw your true, authentic self, who would they see?

_____

_____

_____

_____

_____

_____

_____

_____

_____

_____

_____

_____

_____

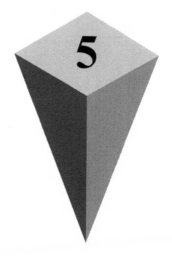

# PUT DOWN THE POISON

*The world needs your hustle.*
*The road is long.*
*Doubts and fears will crowd your mind.*

Can we all agree that some days life sucks? Some days the idea of hustling and pursuing goals and dreams sounds awful! Wouldn't it be better to simply grab our favorite snack, which of course is chips and queso or anything chocolate, and hit up Netflix? Is there anything better in life?

On bad days, I would rather stuff my face, lay on the couch, and binge watch one of my favorite shows, such as *Breaking Bad*! It is by far in my top five shows of all time.

If you haven't watched it, I give you permission to declare binge watching this epic show your new hustle! Yes, it is that good.

There is nothing wrong with having a day or two like this from time to time. Vacations are good! Rest is necessary! We can't hustle every day or we will burn out and lose focus. But don't get carried away and become permanently etched into those couch cushions with potato chip crumbs falling off your face. This is not cute, people.

The truth is, if the pursuit is too easy, we probably aren't dreaming big enough. If life was always rainbows and unicorns, we probably would not accomplish much. But it would be fun to ride around on a unicorn all day. I digress.

If we go into life believing what we are meant to do is going to be easy, then we are setting ourselves up for failure. There will definitely be days that are hard, but I believe that we can overcome this and continue to push forward.

One of those defining moments for me happened at the age of thirty-four. It was the year I decided to become a first-time homeowner. I had always rented, which was okay, but it was time to experience life with a mortgage. And it just so happened this was the year President Obama gave first-time homebuyers $8,000 in credit.

Coincidence? I think not.

Money talks, people, and I did not need to pray about it. It was time to buy a house. Show me the money!

After looking at what seemed like every house in the city, I found one in a neighborhood I loved. Although buying a house was one of the most stressful things I have ever done, it all worked together for good. In December of that year, I became a first-time homeowner! Nothing like getting it done at the last minute, right? I was not going to miss out on that money!

December was great. I loved my new home and purchased all the things to make it how I wanted. January came around, and by the end of that month, I was let go at my job. Talk about a record scratch moment in life. I went home that day, sat on my brand new comfortable couch I had bought, in my new home I had just purchased and thought— oh bleep!

Thankfully, Obama paid me the $8,000 credit the following month, but I would end up going eight months without a job. My hustle quickly shifted.

This is a good reminder for all of us. Many times life does not always agree with our hustle plans and we have to adjust accordingly. And this is okay.

Towards the end of those eight months, I felt like giving up. I was out of money, my car had been taken away from me, and I was worried that I would lose my house. If you have ever experienced deep financial frustrations, you understand how stressful this can be. It's not something you want to talk about, and it is embarrassing if anyone asks what you do for a living.

Saying that you are unemployed always leads to the pity look, which then makes you want to punch them in the throat, and so you try to put a positive spin on it.

"Yes, I am unemployed, but I am using this time to really find myself."

"Being unemployed gives me more time to meditate."

"I love having all this free time!"

Sure, none of it is true, but if it moves the conversation towards something else, then it's a win-win for everyone.

Even though my days were not fun, I kept making the decision to keep the right perspective. I chose determination instead of despair. I believed that change was coming. That life was *for* me and not against me. Again, that attitude wasn't manifested every day, but I knew I had a choice. I was not going to choose to give up.

After eight months, I landed a job. Talk about a happy day!

In the end, things worked out. I still live in the same house and sit on that same couch (maybe it's time for a new couch) and I learned many things from that experience.

I share this with you to encourage you. During that time, my hustle was to find a job and there were definitely moments I wanted to give up. I think many times, the fact that giving up really is not an option helps us to continue. I know it did for me.

Maybe your setback will not be as bad as mine. I hope it isn't. What we all have in common though, is that there will be setbacks in our hustle.

## WHEN THE BAD TIMES ROLL

What is your reaction to setbacks? How do you instinctively handle frustrations? For many of us, we want to throw our hands up and quit! Where are the chips and queso? And the chocolate?

The moment things start to get hard, we want to stop. Many times we will justify it enough that we feel okay with waving the white flag.

The pity party starts and it is a party for only one. Who wants to go to a pity party, right? It's the most depressing party ever. For most of us, we don't care. We will attend our

> # Go ahead and have your pity party. Make it quick, get it out of your system, and then take a step towards moving forward.

party of one and throw pity confetti up in the air, play pity music, and eat pity food.

It's not cute people. It's not cute at all.

Here's what I tell myself when it comes to pity parties: Go ahead. Throw yourself a tantrum if it is what you need. Make it quick, get it out of your system, and then take a step towards moving forward.

## OVERCOME THE ROADBLOCKS

What sets the people who accomplish goals apart from those who do not is in how they handle setbacks. Many dreams and goals have fallen by the wayside because they stopped after the first obstacle. What would the world have missed out on if others had stopped because of a little defeat?

Walt Disney was fired from the Kansas City Star in 1919 because, his editor said, he "lacked imagination and had no good ideas."

Oprah Winfrey was an evening news reporter and was fired because she couldn't sever her emotions from her stories.

Elvis Presley was told by the concert hall manager at Nashville's Grand Ole Opry that he was better off returning to Memphis and driving trucks.

Kerry Washington was replaced in two pilot episodes before she landed the role on Scandal.

Lucille Ball was considered a B-list failed actress and

was told by her drama instructors to find a new profession before her iconic show *I Love Lucy* started.

The list goes on.

All of these people had something in common—they did not let setbacks define them. They believed in their dreams and kept going even when others were telling them to stop. It takes determination, bravery, and courage, but their experiences confirm that setbacks will happen. We can all be thankful that Oprah did not let a small defeat stop her!

It's how we respond to setbacks that makes the difference.

I think for many of us, the problem lies in comparing where we are now to where others are. We see someone living out a dream or accomplishing a goal and it motivates us to get started with ours. We are ready! We get the supplies. We start with a clean sheet of paper. We sign up for that gym membership. We make that phone call. Those initial feelings are so good. We tell everyone about it!

Then it starts to take work and we cannot seem to figure out why our life does not look like theirs.

We forget one tiny but very important detail. It took them time and hard work to get to where they are! They had to put in the work. They had to fail and succeed. They went through setbacks, but found the motivation to keep going!

Although we hear all the time about "overnight successes," the truth is they really never happen. It would be great to wake up and be a superstar or a best-selling author! It would be awesome to lose all the weight in a day or to have our dream job handed to us on a silver platter! How amazing would it be to wake up to a clutter-free, spotless house?

Our goals and dreams rarely happen overnight. They did not happen for others that way and they probably will not happen for us.

Sorry to be such a party-pooper.

What we need to remember is how many people have worked through the frustration and gone on to accomplish awesome things! The setbacks in no way mean that it's over. The moments which do not go exactly as planned should not make us question our entire existence.

It is okay to have hard times. I would say it is good to have those days because it means our goals and dreams are worth putting in the effort and going the extra mile!

Let's get the party started again! Crank up the confetti cannons!

## HOW TO HANDLE THE HARD DAYS

There are different ways to handle the hard days without giving up. For some, it means you need to step away from your hustle for a short time, and that is okay. Sometimes stepping out of the situation gives us a new perspective. My advice is to not step away for too long. Time away can give us a new outlook, fresh eyes, and a renewed energy to get back in the pursuit.

One of the greatest obstacles to not fulfilling our own hustle is the voice that resonates in our own mind. We start to believe the lies that we aren't good enough and give in to the trap of comparison. If you are like me, the voices in our head can get the best of us from time to time. The problem is many times we keep that voice in our mind and allow it to grow like a cancer that seeks to kill our dreams.

How do we overcome this?

Tell someone. Say it out loud.

When you do, the villain loosens its grip and the words which seem to be so powerful will begin to show itself for what they truly are.

Lies.

Here's what I have learned—the negative voices in my head seem to be loud and dominant until I tell someone else about it. Not only do the voices seem to get quieter, but the problem doesn't seem to have as much power. Once I tell someone, I realize I was getting carried away and not clearly seeing the situation for what it was.

> **What sets the people who accomplish goals apart from those who do not is in how they handle setbacks.**

When you tell someone, you start to feel better because it is out there in the open. It may not mean there is an immediate solution but venting to someone helps. It calms you down. You can think about the situation more clearly and can breathe easier.

Don't let the voice win. Do not let disappointment fester. Let the power of saying it out loud clear away the fog so you can continue living the life you were meant to live.

Yes, the difficult days will come and giving up will seem easier than continuing. It is part of the hustle. Continuing the pursuit will show you that it was worth it. The struggle will add to your story. It will make the end result so much sweeter.

Keep hustling friends. Your goal is worth it. Your dream is worth it. You are worth it.

# WRITE IT DOWN:

Be honest. What is your natural reaction to a setback?

_____

_____

_____

_____

_____

_____

_____

_____

_____

_____

_____

_____

_____

# WRITE IT DOWN:

What setbacks in your life have prevented you from accomplishing your goals and dreams?

_____

_____

_____

_____

_____

_____

What is one thing you can do today to turn a setback into progress?

_____

_____

_____

_____

_____

_____

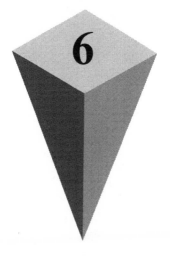

# THREE-LETTER WORDS

*Remember why you hustle*
*and who your life could change.*
*Let the passion to serve be your inspiration*
*and strength to see the journey through.*

This is one of my favorite parts! There are two three-letter words which are the most important words in this book! It makes me really excited to watch others grasp and connect to them.

In my own life, this first three-letter word allowed me to accomplish more than I ever imagined.

The *why*.

The struggle is real. No one ever said living a fulfilled life would be easy. Accomplishing your goals takes work. Living out your dreams isn't always fun. When the hard days happen, where do we find strength? Where is the motivation going to come from when we feel like giving up?

The why. That's where.

Goals and dreams are futile if there is no why behind it. The why gives it meaning, depth, and longevity. Defining the why will keep us motivated when we want to give up. You need to have a strong why behind every goal you pursue. The deeper we get into our goal we might discover a deeper why as well.

If your goal is to get in better shape and live a healthier life, there is a why behind this decision. It not only gives you better quality of life but plays a part in allowing you to be around longer for your loved ones.

I know many parents who have found the why in maintaining control of their health because they want to be around to see their kids grow up. And not only be around, but be able to be active and enjoy the time with them.

Sometimes the why for our goal starts to connect with others and causes us to dream bigger.

Corie Clark has seen this play out in her life in a big way. I met Corie through the *Dreamers and Builders* Facebook group. We quickly became friends and connected over our love of helping people live better lives...and our love for margaritas. Possibly an emphasis on the second one.

Corie is married, a mom, a homeschool teacher, and stays very busy. She began to see the need to simplify her life in order to find balance. In order to make her family a priority, she had to find ways to declutter.

In doing so, she began to see how she could help others do the same. She wrote a book called *The Simplicity Project: Win your Battle with Chaos and Clutter So You Can Live a Life of Peace and Purpose*. In it, she explores four areas of life which need simplifying: health, home, finances, and time.

She gives practical advice which can be applied to each area and helps you find the results you've been looking for.

What I loved about this book was that Corie wrote about her own experience. She was not telling people to do anything she hadn't already done. She even included a 28-day challenge with tasks to help you get in there and win the war against clutter.

This book sold quickly and out of the book she developed a Facebook group by the same name which quickly grew to well over 2,000 members! People loved sharing ideas of how they simplify their own lives. It was a community.

> # People connect more with those who show action than those who continue to merely talk about it.

Shortly thereafter, her online community began showing an interest in a planner. Corie had always wanted to develop her own planner because all the ones in the store never really met her needs. Up until now she never found the motivation to follow through with the idea.

As more and more people showed interest, Corie knew this would be the next step in her dream. She had no experience in design and had no idea how to actually turn this idea into an actual planner people could use.

This did not stop her. She researched and taught herself every step of the way. After months of planning and lots of hustle, The Purposeful Planner® became a reality! It was a huge success and word of mouth praise spread quickly. She now has various forms of the planner available and ships to customers all over the world.

Corie Clark knows the meaning of hustle. It was not easy and there were many frustrating moments along the way, but Corie's passion and desire to help others helped carry her through. She continues to work hard to keep her business going and explore new options and I could not be more proud of her!

What I love about Corie's story is that she turned a problem in her life into something awesome. She took an issue which so many of us deal with (trying to find more balance and simplicity in our lives) and instead of continuing to complain about it and allow it to overcome her life, she took action and did something about it.

People connect more with those who show action than those who continue to merely talk about it. And aren't we attracted more to those who do something about it over those who whine about it?

Out of this connection of helping others, Corie was able to build a business. She could have waited around and let the opportunity pass her by, but she didn't. She chose to take a need people had and help them.

What can we learn from this? Sometimes our dreams and goals are forming in our lives when we least expect it. Taking experiences we have learned from in life and finding ways to share this with others can lead us to opportunities we never knew existed. Corie's story is a true example of how this works.

## BUILD UP SPEED

As we accomplish goals and live out our dreams, we will notice momentum building and other opportunities presenting themselves. Go after them! Seek out those building blocks and ways you can expand.

Writing a blog could lead to writing a book.

Training for a 5k could lead to signing up for a half marathon.

Creating a simple how-to video could lead to a YouTube channel.

Successfully decluttering your house could lead to helping others do the same.

Baking desserts for your neighbors could lead to starting your own business.

Don't think that because you accomplish one goal, you should stop there. Look for ways to build upon your accomplishment and dream bigger!

A little piece of advice: Don't get too ahead of yourself. Just because one thing goes great does not always guarantee all future projects will. Be smart about how you build on momentum. Ask for feedback from those in the same field, try it out in small doses, and do what makes sense.

How to handle momentum is similar to a successful movie. Audiences loved it, the film companies love the profits, and so they start making the dreaded sequel. Or prequel. Or spinoff. And it bombs.

*But I know several trilogies and spin-offs that were fantastic!* Yes, I hear you. And I agree that there are examples of sequels which were even better than the originals. Take *Christmas Vacation* for example. It's a classic and was so much better than the original *Vacation!* It's a must-see movie around the holidays, people!

It just doesn't feel like Christmas without Clark Griswold putting up fifty thousand lights only to have them not work.

Then there's the example of the hilarious movie, *The Hangover.* It was by far the funniest movie of 2009. This was followed by the sequel which got a giggle or two. And then the third one? Come on, it was horrible. There's a way to do it right and a way to do it wrong.

Corie Clark did it right. Her book, *The Simplicity Project,* led to The Purposeful Planner®, and she now has other projects in the works. She listened to the feedback she was receiving and built on the momentum which came from her products.

## SELF-DOUBT

There have been many times I've questioned the quality of my own work. I am guilty of basing my worth on the reaction of others. If I write a blog post and it gets a low number of views or only a few comments, then I think what I wrote was probably crap.

If I share some of my thoughts on social media and only a few people "like" it, then I feel like I need to rethink the direction of my entire life.

Dramatic I know, but it does happen from time to time.

Still, I return to my *why*. Why do I do what I do?

My *why* shows itself when I am able to encourage

someone to believe their life matters and watch them connect this truth to what their life truly means. My *why* comes into play when I can have a conversation with someone and hear their story. It also happens when I speak in front of a group and feel the connection between my words and how it relates to their lives.

> **The why leads us through the tough times and deepens our celebration of the good times.**

I started offering coaching sessions to help others accomplish their goals and fell in love with the one-on-one interaction with people. Even when sessions are held over a Google Hangout or Skype video call, there is an incredible feeling when we start talking about *why* they want to accomplish a particular goal. There is always a deeper reason beneath the surface and I can see the light come on when they connect the why to their goal. When they realize how the accomplishment is not only affecting their life but others as well, it makes all the difference!

Those are moments of clarity when I know I am doing what I was created to do. Everything inside me feels alive and the energy becomes contagious. I feel connected with others and with the bigger picture of how the world works.

The *why* leads us through the tough times and deepens our celebration of the good times.

I cannot stress enough the importance of knowing your why when it comes to hustling toward your goals and dreams in life. Give your why the freedom to change and evolve.

## *WHY* HAS A PARTNER

The second three-letter word is just as crucial as the first.

The *who*.

This life is not just about us. It is not about meeting only our needs. If our eyes are focused on ourselves, we miss out on a world which needs our influence, our ideas, and our hustle. The motive behind this book is to broaden the perspective of our lives and remember that it's not only about us.

While writing this book, I thought many times about the *who*.

No, not the band (although they are awesome), but "the who" as in *you*.

I didn't write this book simply for myself; I wrote it for YOU and for many others with the hope that it provides the extra push to keep hustling on your goals and dreams.

I believe when you can connect your life to the greater picture of the world, it will open up your heart and broaden your perspective to do even more. You will understand that your life really does have an effect on people.

I also thought about those whom I have a direct and tangible effect on.

I am thankful for my two nieces and my nephew who have made the world a much brighter place simply by being who they are. As they grow and get older, I want them to look at "KK's" life and know they can do whatever they want with their life. I want them to know that I strive to make the most of life, to enjoy it, and to know I have a purpose in being here.

And as they grow to be adults, I cannot wait to see how their dreams are formed and the paths they take to discover how they too, can make a difference in this world.

When we think of the *who*, we need to think past our own lives as well. We have the potential of making a difference which continues past our short time here on earth. If we are honest, we will realize it is not a matter of *if* we will be remembered, but *what we will be remembered for.*

I want others to look back on my time here on earth and continue to be encouraged to live a full and meaningful life. They will be encouraged to know while I was far from perfect, there were many struggles along the way. However, I knew what my life was meant to accomplish. I captured my dream and was able to live it out the best way I knew how.

My desire is also to bring glory to the One who created me and encourage others to know this life was not only about me, but rather pleasing God and fulfilling the purpose He birthed in me. It all started with Him and it will end with Him.

Take a minute and think about the who in your life.

Who are the people that are directly affected by your goals and dreams? How would they be affected if you gave up and settled for a life of mediocrity?

Who are the ones who could potentially be impacted by you fulfilling your purpose?

You have to keep going for them.

This is one of my favorite parts because we really never know the full extent of this answer. What I do know is that you will make a difference in ways you may never know. There could be times someone will contact you about something you did or said and it inspired them or caused them to make a shift in the way they thought. A small action can make a big difference in the direction of someone's life.

The greatest example of this came from my dad. He knew what his life was meant for and that was to serve others. He never craved the spotlight or wanted recognition for what he did. For him, it was simply about helping others and understanding that their life was the same as his.

He knew that small acts of kindness could make a big impact on anyone. He would stop and help someone on the side of the road. At Christmas, he always made sure we provided presents to families in need. He was the one raking leaves at homes of the elderly. Or helping with a house repair for a neighbor. If there was an opportunity to do good for others, my dad was the first in line.

In 2004, Dad passed away from a brain tumor. He was the rock in our family and it was the worst to see him go. But

I will never forget being at his visitation on the night before his funeral and as my family and I stood by his casket, there was a steady stream of people for over four hours to come and show their support. Every person had a story of how my dad's life had impacted them.

> # Who are the ones who could potentially be impacted by you fulfilling your purpose? You have to keep going for them.

What stood out the most to me were the ones I had never met before. They told us they had only met my dad once and he had helped them in some kind of way. His kindness made such a difference in their life that when they heard of his passing, they had to come and share. We never knew because Dad didn't tell us. He helped others because that was what he was meant to do. And because he lived out his authentic purpose, he gave others the belief that they could do more with their lives.

Even years after Dad died, I still hear stories of how he impacted others. Did my dad know his purpose in life? Yes. Did he strive every day to live in authenticity and be the person he was created to be? Yes. My dad hustled after his goals and dreams. Even when he struggled in life, he kept going. And in doing so, he forever impacted our lives and those he only met once. The world definitely needed his hustle.

## YOUR COMMITMENT

The *why* and the *who* are what will keep your hustle going. When days come that you don't believe in yourself, the *why* and the *who* will pick you up and carry you one step further. Your goal will not seem as small or insignificant anymore.

Please know this. Your goals, your dreams, your life are never insignificant. Too many times we feel this way when comparing what we do to others' lives. Remember, you were never meant to be compared to someone else. You were never meant to live their life. You were meant to live out your own life and understand that your piece of the puzzle is just as important as the next.

Time spent comparing is wasted time. You are supposed to be you because that is how you were created. When you think about the why and the who, the world doesn't need a copycat. It needs the authentic version of you.

There is always a why to your goals and dreams. There is always a bigger and deeper reason for why we should accomplish our goals and live out our dreams. Do whatever it takes to remind yourself of the *why*. Write it down. Refer to it often.

When you think about the *who*, remember those in your

life who will directly benefit from your goals and dreams. Remember there will be those who you affect that you may never know about. You can probably think of someone who has inspired and motivated you, but they will never know.

The same will be true for your life.

Let this serve as your motivation and strength to keep going.

# WRITE IT DOWN:

What areas have you been talking about for a long time and now it is time for action?

_____

_____

_____

_____

_____

Write down moments in your life that were full of clarity when you knew you were doing what you were created to do.

_____

_____

_____

_____

_____

_____

# WRITE IT DOWN:

What do you want to be remembered for?

_____

_____

_____

_____

_____

_____

_____

_____

_____

_____

_____

_____

_____

_____

# EXCUSES ARE NOT A PRETTY COLOR ON ANYONE

*Dream. Sacrifice. Commit.*
*Rise early; stay up late.*
*Do whatever it takes to make your dreams happen.*
*Take your next step.*

Living out your dreams, accomplishing your goals, and being who you are meant to be is not an easy road to take. It takes persistence, determination, and a willingness to put in the work. The hustle is never something to take lightly. In fact, it may not be for everyone.

It requires sacrifice. Let's start with time. If you have an active social life, this may require sacrificing some of your social time in order to create space to put in the work. If you love TV, you might have to give up some of your shows and use this time to hustle instead. Or maybe giving up cable all together is what you... wait a minute, this is crazy talk!

If you want to see how time is affecting your hustle, try this exercise. For one week, keep track of everything you do. There's even an app for that! ATracker, Reporter, and Hours are some of my favorites. You can also go old school and simply write it down. However you do it, be honest. Keep track of every little thing you do. At the end of the week, go back and see how you are spending your time.

> # Don't let time be an excuse which keeps you from living out your best life.

You will probably be surprised at the amount of time you actually have in this "crazy busy life" we love to tell others we lead. Truth is, we will make time for what is important to us.

Here comes the tough love. Stop making excuses. Stop

saying you are sooooo busy. Make time for your hustle. Don't let time be an excuse which keeps you from living out your best life. And another thing, no one is going to feel sorry for you if you "don't have the time."

There are single moms working two jobs, and raising their kids while still hustling on their goals and dreams. There are people who have gone through unimaginable loss and hurt in their life and yet they have made the decision to still use their time to do something more with their life. There are college kids going to school, working crazy hours, and still finding time to live out their dreams and make a difference.

What's your excuse?

No one gets a pass when it comes to time. Again, you will find time for that which is important to you, so do it.

Maybe the extra time you need is actually happening before the sun comes up.

That's right. Maybe you need to get up earlier. Remember that I mentioned In January of 2013, I started getting up at 5 AM and it made a noticeable difference in my hustle. I was able to spend the first hour of everyday writing.

As it turns out, I am much more productive at writing early in the morning. Once the extra bold, dark roast coffee starts coursing through my veins, my little fingers start typing away. I grew to love it and now it is my favorite part of the day. It seriously is the hour I look forward to the most!

I also understand for some of you, 5 AM sounds like torture. But what if you tried it? Research shows that a large majority of people who are successful are also early risers. Coincidence? I think not.

If you aren't normally wired to be an early bird, then it will take some time to transition, but you never know. You might actually find it to be quite productive and, dare I say, enjoyable! And yes, the coffee helps!

Maybe you are a night owl and need to stay up a little later at night to get the work done. I will admit after about 9:00 PM, I am pretty worthless when it comes to anything which requires focus or brain cells. However, I know plenty of people who work best after the rest of us have given up and gone to bed. If this is you, then I say hustle into the midnight hour!

For those of you with families, getting up early or going to bed late may be the only way you can hustle on your goals and dreams. It is definitely a sacrifice, but those moments of quiet might be exactly what you need to find balance between hustle and family.

Only you know what is best when it comes to managing personal time. Be intentional about it. We all have twenty-four hours and it is up to us as to how they are spent.

## OTHER WAYS TO SACRIFICE

Sacrifice might require a change-of-thought in how you use your finances. You can start by cutting out your daily latte/espresso/overpriced coffee so you can use the money to help accomplish your goal. Brown bag your lunch in order to build your savings. It might even require something more drastic like downgrading your car or selling the expensive home in order to get out of debt. Sure, it sounds crazy, but I know people who have done exactly that in order to speed up the process of doing what they are meant to do.

The question is—how bad do you want it?

I am the first to admit financial smarts have not been my forte in life. I have learned the hard way what it means to not budget, live outside of your means, and not learn to effectively save. I am also the first to say being in debt is a big hindrance to living out your dreams. Nasty debt looming over you will steal your focus. Financial burden is a weight which will continually push you down until you do something about it.

I encourage you to do what it takes to get out of debt. As I have taken measures to improve my financial situation, I found much more freedom to pursue my goals.

For some, you need to stop using people as your excuse. I am going to tread lightly here, but I believe too many times we hide behind others in order to justify not pursuing our own goals and dreams. We camouflage ourselves in the name of supporting a spouse, raising a child, helping a friend, or being stuck in a job we hate and not having support from friends and family.

Again, before you start sending hate mail, I want you to understand what I am saying. I am not a parent, therefore I cannot speak on parenting. And yes, I know great parents do sacrifice parts of their own lives in order to effectively raise great kids. I know this because I had two parents who did exactly that.

What I have observed are those who decide their own dreams will never happen because they have kids. They somehow convince themselves that in order to support their spouse in their dreams, they must turn a blind eye to their own life. Maybe a close friend has a similar idea as you, so you give up on yours in order to help them pursue their idea.

What happens is we lose ourselves in others and then justify it with words like "sacrifice" and "selflessness." We almost want to be looked at with admiration that we would give up our own lives in order to better the lives of someone else.

But are you really the hero?

OK, maybe I'm not treading so lightly anymore.

Yes, there are times we have to sacrifice for others. For the good of our significant others, children, friends, and coworkers we have to temporarily lay aside our pursuits in order to help them reach theirs.

I get it. Trust me, I do.

However, I want to encourage you to not believe the lie that you have to completely give up your dreams and goals. I have a hard time believing this is the way it's supposed to be. You have every right to live the life you are meant to live. You deserve it!

Yes, help others! I have said many times already that we are all connected and I believe we should use our lives to help others reach their potential. This is what most of this book is about. However, these pages are also about living the life you were meant to live. You need to believe you are worth all that life has to offer. Hold to the truth that your life was created with a purpose. It was planned with goals and dreams which were tailor-made for you.

> # You need to believe you are worth all that life has to offer.

Fulfilling your purpose affects how others fulfill theirs. How will the next person be affected if you are not fulfilling yours? There's a break in the ripple which wasn't supposed to happen.

Give yourself permission to do whatever it takes to make your hustle a reality. Only you know what this involves, but you have to believe it is okay. You cannot allow yourself to be lost in the pursuit of someone else's dreams.

When we are doing what we love, we don't think of sacrifice in a negative way. The pursuit of our goals and dreams starts a fire in us, motivating us to keep going. Yes, there will be days that require real work. This is why I don't believe the saying - do what you love, and you will never work a day in your life. I love what I do, and yet some days it is a lot of work! But it is worth it.

In your pursuit and sacrifice, remember your family. Remember those in your household. They will not always understand why you are asking for time and other forms of sacrifice. You need to create balance and have conversations with them so they can support you and not resent you. Sometimes, you have to put the work aside and put them first.

As much as we want those closest to us to understand and provide support, the truth is they might not always be able to. I believe consistent communication, compromise, and mutual support can help.

## THE NEXT STEP

Take your next step.

Goals and dreams require a level of risk-taking. Let's be honest, this is scary! Not knowing exactly where the next step will take us is very hard, especially for control freaks like myself. Can I get an amen?

Sometimes the next step is hard because we know there is a strong possibility that with it could come a new level of success. As much as we might want this, it can also be unnerving because the risks are greater. More people will see if we fail. More mean comments could come our way.

Don't forget—this next step is what we need. This next step is what we want. This next step could open up opportunities for us that we never saw coming.

This next step will also help others see that if you take the next step, they can, too. It can lead to all kinds of crazy success. This next step can connect you with people you never would have known otherwise. It can be the turning point. I think you get the point.

Does the next step guarantee success? No, but you will never know if you don't try. I can look back at my own life and think, "...if I hadn't chosen to take the next step, I would not be where I am today."

When I wrote the poem, "The World Needs Your Hustle," I could have stopped there. I could have left it as a beautifully hand-lettered print that Rachel did and let it be. However, I knew the next step was to turn it into a book. This book! Because the book will impact people in ways the poem can't.

What is your next step? If you are pursuing your goals and living out your dreams, what is the next step you need to take? What is holding you back? Maybe for some of you your next step is actually your first step. You

> **The next step could open up opportunities for us that we never saw coming.**

know what your goal or dream is and now it is time to take the first step.

The first step can sometimes be the hardest, but I want to encourage you to reconsider that perspective. Many times the first step can be easy because it's not on the grand stage. Oprah's first step was not on a television show broadcast to millions of people. It was the small step of sending a resume to a local news station. Steve Jobs' first step was not showcasing an iPhone before the world. It was building a computer in his garage.

Take the pressure off of your first step and the rejection will not be as great. Sign up for the college course. Audition for the part. Write the first chapter. Make the phone call. Just do it. Don't overthink it. Take the first step.

We worry too much about the "what if's" when the truth is the what if's will take care of themselves once we proceed forward with the next step. It probably won't be as bad as we thought it would be.

Yes, your goals and dreams will require some sort of sacrifice, no matter what. It might be a small sacrifice or a big one, but when you are living out your best life, the sacrifice will be worth it.

When you are impacting others, the next step will have been worth it.

When you hear of someone who started hustling on their own goals and dreams because they watched you, it will make those early or late hours worth it.

You life matters. Their lives matter. Yes, by all means do whatever it takes to make it happen.

# WRITE IT DOWN:

What do you need to temporarily sacrifice in order to
accomplish your goals and dreams?

_____

_____

_____

_____

_____

Are you blaming anyone else for your lack of
accomplishment? If so, what steps should you take to correct
this?

_____

_____

_____

_____

_____

_____

# WRITE IT DOWN:

What is your next step?

_____

_____

_____

_____

_____

_____

_____

_____

_____

_____

_____

_____

_____

# THE RIPPLE EFFECT

*Because the world needs your hustle.*

My hope in writing this book is that you would begin to see how your life fits into the bigger picture of this world. In and of yourself, you are significant. Your life matters. Those three words will make all the difference in how you live your life.

Even your dreams and goals do not define who you are. They allow you to live a fuller and more meaningful existence, but we must remember to never fall into the lie that our worth is dependent on whether or not we fulfill them.

When you take away all of the stuff—your titles, the different hats you wear, your occupation, your successes and failures—when you strip it all away and are simply left with the rawest version of yourself, remember your life matters. You are enough and that is beautiful.

## ZOOM OUT

Our identity is found in who we are, not what we do. Be sure to zoom in and find the truth. It helps everything else make sense.

When you zoom out and see how your life connects with countless others, it should increase your motivation and desire to live out the fullest expression of your life. The decisions you make, the choice to live out your purpose or give up...it all affects someone other than yourself.

It *always* affects someone other than yourself.

In fact, it affects more people than you or I will ever

realize. In some ways, all the pressure can cause moments of freaking and stressing out! It is as if the fate of the world is resting on whether or not we hustle towards our goals. It all starts to get very dramatic. However, it is also very narcissistic to think we have that much power.

Let's take a step back, shall we?

---

# Your life matters.

---

Instead of seeing it as pressure, see it as fuel to truly make the most of this one shot at life. See your life as a piece of a much larger puzzle. When you reflect on how you have been influenced by the way others live their lives, the same is true of how they are influenced by yours.

For me, this is such an awesome thought! It is a much deeper and enticing way to look at our dreams, our goals, and our lives. It is not simply about us; it is about affecting others.

## WHAT IF YOU SAID NO?

For the majority of this book, I have encouraged you to hustle. I have done my best to persuade you to see the importance of living out your goals and dreams. But what if you don't do it? What if you decide to give up and simply live the life you have now?

What if you said no?

You would probably go on to live a good life. You would wake up and do what you've always done. Your family and friends would still like you. You would have everything you have now. And you wouldn't have to worry about the unknown or the "what could have been's" because it won't matter.

But do you really want to settle for only what you have now? Would you be truly content living the life that only serves the purpose of you? I can't help but think of all that you would miss out on. And what all the world would miss if you didn't pursue all that your life is meant for!

I want you to pursue more because your life matters. When we say NO, we are screaming out that we are not worth it. We are letting fear win.

I once heard someone say that every time we say no to what know we are supposed to do, we are throwing more dirt on our grave. This is not the life we are meant to live. I want you to believe with everything you have that your goals and dreams matter. And I want you to not rest until you try.

The rest of the world deserves to experience the fullest expression of yourself you can give. Not only do they deserve it... they need it. They need that extra push to believe in themselves. Your family needs to see you saying YES. Your friends need to hear you saying YES with your life.

The next generation needs to be brought up to believe in the possibilities of their life because they saw us say yes to ours. Just as my grandparents taught me the power of hard work, determination, and a belief that our life is meant for great things, I must do the same for those who come after me.

If we want the ripple effect to continue in a positive way, we must say YES! Think about it. If you come from a history of those who said NO to life, it begins to be ingrained in your life early on. It takes a lot of work and a complete change of mindset to rise above. It's not impossible but you have to work hard to break the cycle.

If this is you, I hope you make the intentional decision to say YES. To decide your life will be different not only for yourself, but for the generations that come after.

Could you say no? Sure, the choice is yours. But think about what saying YES will mean for you life and for the world.

The purpose for your life was given to you for a reason. It fits perfectly with who you are. It was tailor-made specifically for you. The dreams you have will not go away because they are meant to be expressed. Using the excuse that someone else will do it won't work anymore. Sure, they might get close, but no one else can live out the fullest expression of your life except for you. And no one else can impact others the way you can. It is bigger than you and yet it is meant for you. Your life connects with others every single day.

Everything you need to live out the life you were created for is already inside you. It has been there all along. It is not a game that life is trying to play where it hides our purpose and we have to spend years seeking it out from impossible hiding places.

It is right in front of us.

It is inside us.

It is all around us.

It is happening now. We simply need to get quiet, clear out the clutter, and listen to the voice inside telling us which way to go.

You fulfilling your dream affects the next person fulfilling theirs. Do not let this idea get by you. Grasp the magnitude. I have seen many people experience their goals and dreams on a new level when they understand that there is a world out there that needs them to hustle and make it happen!

Perhaps you are wondering whether or not you should take those first steps. You may be in the thick of it, frustration has caused doubt, and this doubt wants you to quit. Maybe you are living out your dream but know you should take it to the next level. Wherever you are in life, the answer is yes - keep going! It is not only about you. It is about a world out there who needs you.

The answer was always yes.

> # To decide your life will be different not only for yourself, but for the generations that come after.

You see, life is working for us. Too many times we view life as this monster of negativity that is out to ruin us. Is life always easy? No. There are days which are hard and moments will come that will seem like more than we can handle. I believe there is always hope and if we can hold on to that hope, we will get to the other side.

So...your goals and dreams? Yes, they are there for a reason. Yes, they are meant to be lived out. Yes, you were designed to do it. And yes, you have what it takes to accomplish them. You've always had it in you.

Does it require hustle? Yes! It will require you to work harder than you ever have. It will take you to places, emotions, and experiences you never knew were possible. There will be days that completely drain you, and then you will be required to wake up the next morning and do it all over again.

But guess what? There will also be days that are so much fun you cannot believe this is what you actually do! There will be "a-ha moments" and it will all make sense. There will be a time when you wake up before your alarm clock because you cannot wait to get started! There might even be a time when you stay up until crazy hours of the night hustling because you have lost track of time. And yes, for me that's anytime after 9:30 PM!

You are living out your dream! You will look back at what you thought was impossible and not only was it possible, it has now become your life.

You will hear from people who are impacted by the way you are living your life. Not only have you become a better person, but others have found inspiration. They have found that spark. They are now pursuing the dream they could not get away from.

I bet someone did this for you. Now you are doing it for someone else. It's the beautiful picture of how this world works. We can't begin to understand the fullness of how we are all connected. But this is how it is supposed to work. What brings us together is what makes us human. There is no better place than living the life you were meant to live. It will open you up to opportunities you never thought possible. It will bring people into your life who will walk with you, encourage you, and cheer you on.

The fact that you are reading this book is the result of a realization in my own life that the world needs my hustle. I knew writing this book would not be easy. Sure, the ideas were there and I do enjoy writing. Writing about a topic I am passionate about makes it somewhat easier.

However, the process of writing a book is not always easy. There are days I simply did not want to write. I could think of a hundred other things I would rather do, but then I remembered all of you. I knew there were others who needed to hear this.

There are many who have impacted me because of their obedience. I could write an entire book on those people alone. Now, I must do my part to keep it going. I want to be a part of the ripple effect.

I know there will be people who I may never meet, but they will pick up a copy of this book and be encouraged to keep going. This book will play a part in their journey. I realized the bigger picture of what I was doing and it kept my fingers typing away at the keyboard.

Do you see how it works?

Do you see how it all fits together?

Other people hustled and inspired me to live out my own dreams. I hustled and have motivated others to hustle. It is a ripple effect that goes farther than we know. It really is a beautiful thing in life.

You are meant to do the same. Stop asking questions. Stop allowing the doubt to win. Do not compare yourself to others. You have something unique to bring to the table.

> # You will look back at what you thought was impossible and not only was it possible, it has now become your life.

## NO TIME LIKE THE PRESENT

Let this start now.

Whatever job you have today, approach it with the idea that you are making a difference. You are impacting lives.

Don't wait for your dream job to happen before you find meaning in what you do.

As you "do life" with your family and friends, remember they need you *now*. Yes, your future goals and dreams will inspire them, but how you live your life today will show them what matters.

Because moments matter. Being able to live in the moment and be present is something we all can work on. How you choose to live your life today will be the compass that leads you into the future. It all matters.

Start today.

Your life matters. Your goals, your dreams, your passions. Do it! Do not give up. You were meant to do this and I believe you can.

## FINAL THOUGHTS

I believe in you. Those are not words I say lightly. I may not know you, but I do believe in you. How can I say that? Because I know that every life matters. I know that every life is created for a purpose. And I want to believe in that with everything I have. I know the importance of having someone who believes in you. I hope you have someone like this, but if you do not, then please know that I. Believe. In. You.

Don't do it only for yourself. Remember there are others who need you to live out your dreams so that they will find the inspiration to live out theirs.

I hope this book will help you live a better life, whether it was through a chapter, a sentence, or one word. I hope you close your eyes, take a deep breath, and pursue life with everything you have.

You are meant for all this world has to offer. Others who know of your life will be encouraged and understand they, too, are meant for more.

Do it for them.

Keep going.

Because my friend, the world need your hustle.

# WRITE IT DOWN:

What would it mean if you said NO to your goals and dreams?

_____

_____

_____

_____

_____

_____

Who are the people that are affected by your goals and dreams being accomplished?

_____

_____

_____

_____

_____

_____

# WRITE IT DOWN:

What do you need to get started on today to live the life you were meant to live?

_____

_____

_____

_____

_____

_____

_____

_____

_____

_____

_____

_____

_____

# BONUS SECTION

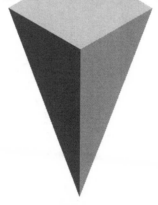

## MAKE YOUR GOALS AND DREAMS MATTER: THE 4-STEP PLAN

A majority of this book is spent telling you why you should hustle on your goals and dreams. I believe the *why* is vital to you living accomplished goals and dreams. I also fully believe in the deeper reason why you should live the life you are meant to live. Your life matters and your life affects how the next person lives theirs.

And when you connect to the bigger reason of why your life matters, you find the motivation to pursue goals. You are inspired to live out the dreams life has given you. And that is awesome!

I felt like I would be doing you a disservice if I did not carry this idea one step further. All the motivation in the world does no good if you don't take the first step and begin a plan. It's like wanting to get in shape. You can believe that you want to all day long. You can know how it will improve your life. You can even understand how it will impact others. But until you get your butt to the gym, go for a walk, or put on the exercise video, you're never going to get in shape. All the good feelings in the world don't cause the weight to magically fall off or the muscles to just appear.

No matter what the lady on the screen says, there's no magical pill for that. You have to put in the work.

Part of my job includes the title of goal coach. It's very similar to being a life coach, but I'm not fond of that term. I help others accomplish a wide variety of goals in their life and it is one of the most rewarding parts of my job! From personal goals to career goals, I have had the opportunity to work with many different people and see the confidence and excitement that develops when we take a goal, put in the work, and see it through to the finish line.

I have always been a goal-oriented person and over the years have accomplished both big and small goals. As I looked back, I discovered four steps that were involved no matter what goal I was pursuing. It played a key role in me getting goals off the page and into my life. I use this same four-step process with my clients.

I now want to share those with you. I will be the first to admit that you will not be calling me a genius for these ideas. Your jaw will not drop to the floor in amazement that I could uncover these never-before-heard secrets to goal and dream accomplishment. But I don't believe we always need earth-shattering ideas. We simply need to be reminded of the basics. We need a fresh perspective on the fundamentals to give us the motivation to keep going.

However, if you want to tweet me (@_kevinbuchanan) and tell me how these ideas are the most amazing thing you have ever heard before, go ahead. I won't stop you.

My advice is to work through each of these steps. At the end of each section there are places for you to write. Those lines aren't there for decoration. They are meant to help you put action to your words. No matter how big or small you think your goal or dream is, these four steps will help take it out of your head and into the reality of your life.

## 1. GET SPECIFIC

A common mistake made in setting goals is that we make them too broad. We start off with a really big goal that requires lots of different parts and before long we lose motivation. It becomes hard to form a plan or even know where to start. That leads to a big old batch of burnout.

A prime example of this is the biggest goal-setting day of the year: January 1st. We get caught up in the moment and believe that we are the Superman of goal accomplishments! We set these massive goals! Big dreams that sound impressive! Or we come up with 26,975 goals that we want to accomplish through the year! And if you have the nerve to ask us how the heck we think we can do all this, we will punch you in the face and question how you can call yourself a human being! We've got this. We've *so* got this.

Somehow week two comes along and we've made little to no progress. We still talk a big game, but we don't have much to show for it. We can spout off a list of reasons… ahem *excuses*… why we aren't able to make progress. But the truth is the party hats have come off, the glitter is swept away, and the reality of the hustle isn't as appealing to us anymore.

By week three, some mysterious force seduces us to the couch, turns on Netflix, and we decide that maybe we will try again next year.

Let's make it even more personal.

You set a goal that you want to get in shape. You are definitely going to do it this year. You can't wait to start! The problem is, if you set this really broad goal of "getting in shape" and leave it at that, it's probably not going to happen.

Sure, you might have a few good days at the start. You'll walk into the gym and actually pick up a dumbbell. You will only drink sodas in the privacy of your broom closet. You'll speed past the McDonald's instead of being greeted by name at the drive-thru.

You'll feel great about yourself and tell everyone how you are "in shape." Then, something happens and you can't go to the gym. And something else happens and you can't go the next day. There's a lot of "if-only's" and "what had happened was" being tossed around and before you know it, there are empty soda cans lying on the counter and week-old french fries in the floorboard of your car.

What happened? We had such great intentions! This was going to be the year!

The problem is a common one. We set broad goals and never figure out exactly what it is we want to accomplish. We come up with pages and pages of goals but, in our attempt to chase after all of them, we never accomplish any of them.

You have to be specific with your goals. Simplify, simplify, simplify. Instead of saying you want to get in shape, say you want to lose X number of pounds. Say you want to go to the gym X number of times per week. Say you are going to cut out sodas for thirty days. Say you will go for a walk for X number of minutes a day. Whenever numbers or dates can be used in your goal, it's a great thing!

Another reason to get specific is so that you have a clear vision of what the end result will look like. You need to know exactly when you've accomplished the goal.

Let's go back to getting in shape for a minute. With this broad goal, how do you know when you've achieved it? What shape do you need to be in to say you did it? A rectangle, circle, pear, hourglass, what? It's too much! Simplify it. Make your goal specific.

When I am coaching my clients, I tell them to write down their goal. Then write it again and make it specific. And if needed, write it one more time and make it even more specific. I can't stress this enough. When you know exactly what you're hustling after, the rest of the steps will fall into place.

If you are new to goal setting, make it attainable! If the only reason you run is to grab the last piece of chocolate cake in the refrigerator, don't declare a goal that you are going to run a marathon in a month. Sure, you can have a goal to run 26.2 miles, but you might want to train for a 5k first.

Making your goals attainable, especially in the beginning, will set you up for success. Once you accomplish an easier goal you will gain the confidence to try for something more and you can build upon that. But if you start off with a goal that is too ambitious and demanding, you are more likely to fail. And it is much harder to pick yourself up in the beginning and find that much needed momentum to keep going.

When I talk about January goals, I strongly encourage everyone to set very specific and very attainable goals. Why? Because if we accomplish our January goals, we are much more likely to set and accomplish our February goals. If we keep it simple and specific in the beginning, then we are setting ourselves up for success instead of failure. It's hard to get back in the game in February or March when January's goals were a flop.

Get specific with your goals. Break down your big yearly goals into smaller monthly goals. And break those monthly goals into weekly goals. And you might even want to break those weekly goals into daily goals. Dare I say make a few of your daily goals into hourly? When I say small and specific, I mean it!

Do I want you to dream big? Yes! Do I want you to go after goals that are out of your reach? Yes! But I want you to go about it the right way. I've learned this the hard way and I want you to learn from my mistakes. Give it a try. Trust me, you'll thank me later.

Now let's put it into practice. What is a goal or dream you want to hustle towards? Write a general idea of what it involves. Now write it again and see how specific you can get. Do you have a clear vision of what the end result will look like?

## 1. GET SPECIFIC

_____

_____

_____

_____

_____

_____

_____

_____

_____

_____

_____

_____

_____

_____

_____

_____

_____

## 2. DECIDE YOUR WHY

I won't spend a lot of time on this one because the entire book was about this, but for every goal you set, there should be a strong *why* behind it. Many times, the more we talk it through, we will discover deeper *why's* than we even realized. This is where it gets really good.

One of my favorite parts about coaching my clients is when they discover their *why*. Many times they know it but I have literally seen their a-ha moment happen as we talk through why these goals and dreams are meant to be accomplished in their life. It is all there to help us live better lives.

What starts as a goal of decluttering your house turns out to be a direct reflection on your life. Your *why* began as a need to have a cleaner house with less stuff in it. You then discovered your life was full of stuff and in desperate need of decluttering. Your *why* takes on a whole new meaning which in turn creates a stronger motivation to accomplish the goal!

The reason you want to set a goal of getting out of debt seems obvious. No one wants to deal with financial stress. It's the worst. But as you look deeper, you realize that the stress of the debt is not simply weighing on your bank account. It is weighing on your entire life. It is keeping you from effectively pursuing your dreams.

Your *why* deepens. You aren't hustling to simply fill your wallet. You want to fill your life with the things you've always wanted to do.

I want to reiterate the importance of writing down your *why*. It is so important. You will want to refer back to it often, especially on the frustrating days. Let's be honest; when the going gets tough, your *why* won't always be at the forefront of your mind. Which means the tough won't get going anywhere except to the couch. If you don't have it written down, you will find yourself questioning all of life by thinking, "Why the heck am I trying to accomplish this goal again, because right now I have no idea!"

If it is written down, you will put down the poison, look at the beautiful piece of paper, take a deep breath, and remember that yes, what you are pursuing is completely worth it.

Know your why, people.

Let's put this into practice. I want you to write down why you want to accomplish the goal you wrote about in step one. How did this goal come about in your life? What need will it meet when you accomplish it? Why do you want to see it completed? Think about your *why* and see if there is a deeper reason that maybe you hadn't thought about before.

## 2. DECIDE YOUR WHY

_____

_____

_____

_____

_____

_____

_____

_____

_____

_____

_____

_____

_____

_____

_____

## 3. CREATE AN ACTION PLAN

This is where the work comes in. Once you get specific with your goal and connect with your *why*, you need to have an action plan to make it happen. Devise a step-by-step agenda you can easily follow to get this goal over to the side of success!

Again, breaking it down into smaller acts will help you accomplish the bigger goal. Remember, small steps equal big leaps. Completing one smaller part of the goal gets you one step closer to the end. What is it going to take to complete your goal?

I have worked with a few clients on decluttering, organizing, and cleaning their houses. I always love helping others in this area because I love those three words so much - decluttering, organizing, and cleaning!

Many times they want to work on the entire house, but it feels so overwhelming and they don't know where to start. So instead, nothing happens and the problem gets worse instead of better. This is true for many goals. The task is intimidating and you have no clue where to begin. That's understandable. Never fear! Coach Kevin is here!

Here is a real-life scenario of how I work with clients and develop an action plan. We take their entire house and add up the number of rooms that need to be worked on. If the plan is to finish the entire house in a month, we take the total number of rooms and divide it by four. That breaks the total square footage down into smaller, realistic working goals. We might adjust some for room size, but we try to distribute the workload over four weeks.

I then advise my client to go through each room assigned for that week and implement the following plan. Yes, I am giving all of you my top-secret, people-pay-crazy-amounts-of-money, easy-to-follow plan for decluttering, organizing, and cleaning your home. Consider it part of your bonus for purchasing the book. You're welcome!

- Have two bags. One for trash and one for items to donate.
- Go through the room and put things in both bags as needed. This is a great time to simplify and declutter so make intentional decisions about what you will keep and what you can get rid of. If you aren't sure, get rid of it. What would Kevin do? He would say get rid of it!
- Organize everything that remains. Rearrange any furniture. Declutter any shelves. Take care of it now. Do not put it off until later.
- Last call for things to throw away or donate! I dare you to get rid of five more things!
- Cleaning:
  - Go from top to bottom
  - Dust anything on the walls, ceiling fan, light fixtures
  - Dust furniture/shelves/other items
  - Clean windows
  - Clean appliances, sinks, toilets, mirrors
  - Wipe down baseboards
  - Vacuum / Clean floors
- Last call for organization. Want to rearrange anything else?
- Make a wish list of things you would like to do to the room in the future.

Okay, so maybe this isn't top-secret information, but it does create a good action plan to follow. It is straightforward, specific, attainable, and gives you a way to check off the steps as you go. You have a clear vision of what the end result will look like and you have a very visible way to know when you have completed the task.

Whatever your goal, there should be an action plan attached to it. If not, it's simply going to be a lot of talk and no action. That's not attractive, people. Isn't that our highest goal in life anyway? To be seen as attractive? I'm joking. Don't go looking for the receipt now. It's too late, you're almost to the end.

But the truth is, when it comes to goals there are usually two groups of people. Group #1 is full of people talking about their goal. They have a lot to say and it's a very loud group.

Group #2 is made up of those who put action to their words. This group is not as loud because they are out there hustling on their goals instead of hanging out with Group #1 at the local snow cone shop. Although snow cones are delicious, you want to be in Group #2. After you hustle, you can go enjoy that snow cone. I'm sure the "talkers" will still be there anyway.

When it comes to action plans, make sure you work smarter not harder. If you know of someone who has accomplished a similar goal, ask them what worked and what didn't work for them. I do believe that we should learn as we go and not always rely on others but don't waste time making the same mistakes someone else did. As I hustled on this book project, I reached out to many people asking questions, advice, suggestions, feedback, and other random texts that seemed important at the time. It was definitely a learning experience and I gained a lot of valuable knowledge along the way, but I saved myself a lot of time by reaching out to others who have done it well. Sure, some of them may have blocked me from their phone but it's okay.

Always write your action plan down. You need a starting point, a plan of how you will get there, and what the end result will look like. With my coaching clients, I send them an action plan every week. After we discuss what their weekly go will be, I send them a detailed plan of action outlining what they should accomplish for the week, how they will get there, and what the result will be. Again, we can talk all day about what you want to accomplish but until you put action to your words it will never happen.

Here is another piece of advice.. Make your to-do list for the day the night before. This way you go to bed knowing what you have to get done. As you sleep, your brain already begins to work on the plan. And you will wake up with a focused plan of attack for the day.

If you need to adjust your action plan as you go, that is okay. If something isn't working, change it. Make sure and push yourself when needed to get it done. Fifteen minutes of focused hustle can be very productive and beneficial to your goal. And if you need an accountability partner to check in with you, do it. Choose someone who will encourage you but also push you to hustle. Do whatever it takes to make it happen.

An action plan is a necessary step that cannot be overlooked. And when you need that extra push to keep going, remember what the end result will look like. Use the space below to begin drafting your action plan.

# 3. CREATE AN ACTION PLAN

_____

_____

_____

_____

_____

_____

_____

_____

_____

_____

_____

_____

_____

_____

_____

_____

# 4. CELEBRATE YOUR ACCOMPLISHMENT!

Cue the balloon drop and confetti cannons! Break open the champagne! Bust out your best happy dance because it's time to party! Yes, you've got to celebrate when you complete your goal! You deserve it.

At the beginning of your hustle journey, you need to decide what your "Celebrate" will be. It doesn't have to be anything big. Sure, if you want to reward yourself with a trip to Cabo, then by all means do it. Take me with you!

But your special celebrate moment might be your favorite Starbucks drink, or a day at the spa, or an afternoon to yourself. If you and your partner are working towards a goal together, you could reward yourselves with a fun date night once it is accomplished!

It doesn't matter what it is; you need to have some kind of celebration planned from day one. I make my clients decide at the beginning what their *celebrate* will be. And for some, this is the hardest part.

Why? Because they don't feel like they deserve a reward. It all goes back to the fact that many of us struggle with our worth. We would tell anyone else to celebrate their accomplishments but when it comes to us, we say no. Well, Coach Kevin doesn't allow that! And I am telling you now that you deserve to celebrate.

Again, it can cost little to no money at all. But you have to have a reward. It will help keep you hustling on your goals and dreams. Rewards work, people! They have worked on us since we were little kids. How many times did my parents get me to do my chores by offering gold stickers or money? Yes, I was that kid who found great pleasure in getting a gold sticker. Cash money was nice, too.

Treat yo self! You deserve it. You worked hard and deserve a treat. As part of your celebratory moment, let me also encourage you to take a minute to live in the accomplishment. Don't immediately jump to the next goal. You need to embrace the fruition of all that happened. Take at least twenty-four hours, if not longer, to enjoy what you have done and then you can move on to bigger things!

Believe that you are worth it. Declare that you will celebrate your hard work! Write down a few ideas of what your reward could be.

## 4. CELEBRATE YOUR ACCOMPLISHMENT!

_____

_____

_____

_____

_____

_____

_____

_____

_____

_____

_____

_____

_____

_____

_____

_____

## CONCLUSION

There it is. My four-step plan for accomplishing your goals! As I said earlier, it's not brand new information, but it does create a strong foundation which works for any goal or dream you are meant to pursue.

My hope is that this will help take all of your motivation and belief and give you a way to channel it into an accomplishment. Let's not only believe we can, but let's see it through to the end!

# ACKNOWLEDGEMENTS

There are numerous people to thank for playing a part in this project!

My family - thank you for embracing me at my best and at my worst. Your support means the world to me.

Devan - If you looked up *opposites attract* in the dictionary, our picture would be front and center. But I wouldn't change a thing. I love getting to share life with you. Your smile brightens every day and I am truly the lucky one. I love you.

Rachel Mayo - Twinsie! Does anyone else on the planet understand each other like we do? I don't think so and I love you for it! Thanks for always dreaming with me, believing in me, and pushing me to do more. We define soul mates in the best (and most platonic) way possible.

Jon Acuff - thanks for sending out one email that changed my entire life.

The 30 Days of Hustle group - I wrote a poem one night and posted it to the group. Your encouraging comments turned it into what it is today. You all define the word hustle so well!

The #5AMClub - I love you guys so much! Who knew there were others out there who wanted to get up early and hustle on their goals? You inspire and motivate me every morning with how you are changing the world. Thanks!

Ronei Harden - I'm pretty sure you had to buy extra red pens for all the editing this book needed, but I am thankful that you did. Thank you for being in my life.

Corie Clark - I absolutely love dreaming with you! Thank you for reading the millions of texts I sent you during this project asking every possible question imagined. Here's to more margaritas and Malibu Barbie and Oprah World Domination!

Bethany Jett - You are my hero. Thank you, thank you, thank you for all the work you put into this book! All the

FaceTime's, the texts, and the midnight laughs. You are simply the best.

Ben Morton- Your ability to embrace life and live in authenticity will always inspire me to do more. You are such a talented writer and the world needs your hustle. Thanks for your friendship and unique ability to include *manatees* and *sharks* in a text message!

Mike Loomis - You have impacted my life more than you realize. Thank you not only for your endorsement and encouraging words with this project, but for your ability to include a massive amount of wisdom in only a few words.

Andrea Lacy - You have been my accountability partner for so long. But more than that, you are a true and genuine friend and I cannot say thanks enough! I appreciate your strong words of encouragement and hilarious text messages that always brighten my day!

# LEARN MORE

If you want to learn more about any of the stories mentioned in this book, please visit their website and show your support! I am thankful to each of them for allowing me to share how the world needs their hustle.

| Jon Acuff | acuff.me |
| Sarah Harmeyer | neighborstable.com |
| Rachel Mayo | therachelmayo.com |
| Matt Ham | mattham.com |
| Corie Clark | corieclark.com |
| Lauren Athalia | laurenathalia.com |

# ABOUT THE AUTHOR

Kevin Buchanan lives in Nashville, Tennessee, and is a writer, speaker, and goal coach. His message centers around the unwavering truth that your life matters. He believes the goals and dreams in your life are there for a reason and are meant to be lived out now! Kevin is known  for his love of Target, Chick-fil-A, and all things plaid! Visit TheWorldNeedsYourHustle.com to learn more about his work, coaching, and upcoming projects!

If you are interested in booking Kevin for a speaking engagement or would like to purchase bulk orders of this book, please visit TheWorldNeedsYourHustle.com.

You can also reach out via email at kevinbuchanan.me@gmail.com to learn more.

TheWorldNeedsYourHustle.com

38392884R00104

Made in the USA
Middletown, DE
17 December 2016